RUN TO THE RAINBOW

D1495173

JIM DOUGLAS

Jim Douglas

EDITED BY LILLIAN KING

ISBN No: 0 9552788 0 5

ACKNOWLEDGEMENTS

In this slightly fictionalised account of childhood in a mining community, some names and locations have been changed and some characters are composites, but all are based on actual events.

I would like to express my gratitude to:
Lillian King, friend and publisher for her ongoing interest in and support of my work
Bill and Belle Hammond for their valuable advice and assistance
Ron Ferguson for kindly agreeing to write the foreword
Joyce Forrest for her careful enhancement of photographs, adding an extra visual dimension
All those who supplied photographs
And to my wife and family, relatives and friends without whose encouragement and support I could not attempt to reach the rainbow.

Somewhere over the rainbow, bluebirds fly
Birds fly over the rainbow, why then oh why can't I?

(*Somewhere Over the Rainbow* - music by Harold Arlen, lyrics by E.Y. Harburg)

Typesetting, layout and design by Windfall Books
Cover design Belle Hammond, artwork Jim Douglas
Published by Windfall Books
Printed by Nevisprint Ltd, Fort William

FOREWORD

This is an exceptional book by an exceptional man. Jim Douglas, poet, artist and writer, has a keen eye for the telling detail and an acute sense of what is important. His excellent illustrated poetry collection, *Dugs Doos and Dancing,* was a real treasure, and this latest book, *Run to the Rainbow,* is another treat; it is a memoir that will not only make you smile, but laugh out loud. I certainly did.

The story of his grandparents' wedding is an astonishing one – his grandmother thought she was going to the registry office to be a witness at a friend's wedding – and the tales from Jim's childhood in Kelty wonderfully convey the atmosphere of a typical mining community at a time when the coal industry was at its height.

Jim Douglas's engaging writing style ensures that the interest of the reader is maintained throughout. A natural story teller, he artfully paints his word pictures in a way which draws the reader into the action, whether he is describing relatives, classmates, miners, dogs, teachers or fellow workers. There are stories in this book that you will want to go back to again and again.

Run to the Rainbow is a colourful and delightful memoir. I am glad to commend it to you.

Ron Ferguson

Jimmy Jones (left) and friends

THE BURIAL

The hearse crawled slowly like a large black obscene beetle up the steep hill to Kirk o Beath cemetery. Cars followed at respectable intervals. The men on the pavements stood still and removed their bonnets. Women spoke in hushed voices and tried to keep the children quiet. Solemnity hung on the air like a pall of smoke.

I was four years old and knew that the procession was special. Our house stood at the bottom of the brae leading to the cemetery and the cars would pass at least once a week. Such splendour of black immaculate vehicles, polished wood, golden handles and glorious blooms in the drab morning must be something to do with a king, I thought. Since they passed so often, what a lot of kings the mining village of Kelty must have.

"That will be auld Mister Todd," a neighbour whispered to mother, "He's been failing for a while."

I felt a twinge of disappointment. I knew Mr. Todd with his pale face and racking cough. He was no king, I was sure of that. A thin, mangy whippet had trailed at his heel. Kings kept corgis, not whippets. There was no sign of Mr. Todd in the car, only two men, ramrod straight in long black coats beside the driver, gazing straight ahead, ignoring the people on the pavements. A king would have waved, at least.

"Where is Mr. Todd, mother?" I whispered, tugging at her apron.

She hesitated

"He's in that big brown box son, and they're taking him to Kirk o Beath cemetery to be buried in the ground."

"But he won't like that, will he?" I asked anxiously, thinking that even a bad cough and a whippet that walked on three legs preferable to a hole in the ground.

"Well, he's dead, you see, son, and when you're dead you get buried and your soul goes to heaven."

Dead ? Soul? I pondered. I knew what dead meant, I had found a sparrow in the back garden, stiff and cold with closed, empty eyes. Pud had told me it was dead. But soul? There was no sign of that unless it was the black burrowing thing in the feathers, scurrying into the grass at my probing fingers.

"You'll understand better when you're older," my mother said as she gathered me into her warm, safe embrace and carried me indoors.

We buried Toe Thomson the following day. His real name was Tommy but everyone called him Toe. He should never have been buried. Some women had families of seven, eight or more children and one buried would scarcely have been missed, but Toe was special, an only child of middle-aged parents and the sun that lit up their lives.

Four of us were playing in a ditch near the Lindsay Pit. Pud, the oldest, boldest and strongest boy, selected the youngest and least resistant for the doubtful privilege.

"Let's bury Toe Thomson," he suggested.

Jackie and I were terrified, but better to bury than to be buried we thought. Toe lay down obediently in the clammy ditch, arms folded across his chest. Pud, who obviously knew about funerals, droned in a monotonous voice "Ashes to ashes, dust to dust," then showing off, rather unsuitably, "and let the body be cast into the sea."

After all, there was only a small trickle of water in the ditch. We piled the body with divots, stones and a rusty bed end, then left

"Have you seen Toe Thomson?" my mother asked me about an hour later. "His mother is looking everywhere for him."

"We gi'ed him a funeral, mother," I said, "Just like Mr. Todd. Pud wis goin tae hit us if we didnae help him."

I led the way followed by mother and Mrs. Thomson. At the ditch the two women tore frantically at the debris and soon mother dragged Toe out, unconscious and bleeding at the nose. Mrs Thomson couldn't bear to look at him and wailed like a lost dog as my mother carried Toe to his home and put him to bed, where he soon recovered. Eck Thomson arrived home from the pit and had to be restrained by his wife.

He threatened to bury Pud for good in retaliation, and had these massive hands found Pud's neck no one would have given tuppence for his chances of survival. Pud's mother defended her offspring vehemently.

"Someone must have put him up to it," she cried accusingly.

Toe grew up to reach over six feet and joined the Scots Guards at eighteen. Jackie and I, perhaps welded together in fear, became inseparable playmates. Pud graduated to school bully.

THE UNDERTAKER

At sixteen years of age I was apprenticed to an undertaker with the Cooperative Society. I stood on a narrow plank, fifteen feet above the ground. Coffins rested on the plank at one end and on a ledge of the wall at the other. My head nearly touched the sarking of the roof, which was covered in cobwebs, and spiders raced for shelter as I brushed the webs with my face.

We were undertakers and joiners and the large evil eye of the circular saw winked under me as its sharp teeth bit viciously into timber while I balanced like a tight-rope walker above. On the floor below, George the Undertaker shouted instructions. He could see the sizes of the coffins written in white chalk underneath. He indicated the box he wanted and I slid a small plank underneath the coffin and pulled it towards me until I could lift it bodily.

I then staggered to the end of the plank, trying to avoid looking down, and passed my burden to George and a journeyman waiting on a raised area at the end of the workshop. It was a relief when this part of the journey was over.

After climbing down the ladder I carried the heavy black pot filled with pitch to an outhouse. This part of the job was pleasant. I lit a gas ring and watched the black lumps sink slowly into the liquid pitch, while a strong delightful smell pervaded the small room.

It had been a macabre morning, with coffins, spiders, black cauldrons, pools of bubbling pitch and, to complete the picture, Nick the vanman, a tall man with piercing blue eyes and a heavy black moustache, was hosing down his vehicle outside. I supposed that they would call him 'Auld Nick' when he retired. There was nothing supernatural about the loud raucous voice shattering my reverie, however.

"Hurry up with that pitch," George the Undertaker roared.

I carried the black pot back to the workshop and poured it slowly into the coffin which George rocked from side to side sealing any possible leaks. Gathering fresh shavings from the bench, I filled the small white pillows and left them on a clean sheet of plywood. My next tasks were to take the brass nameplate to the painting department and cycle round the branches of Kelty Co-operative Society with the black-edged funeral notices.

The branch managers treated me respectfully as the Harbinger of Death, and I was given cups of tea and biscuits to sustain me on my joyless journey. On wet days when work was scarce, I would make tiny coffins for stillborn babies out of rough sarking later to be dressed in white cloth by George.

Death was a joyful affair in the workshop. After an order came in, George and his assistant floated about smiling and whistling. One funeral paid most of the wages for a week and they often received a tip and a large glass of whisky. On a funeral day, George underwent a metamorphosis. In the morning he worked at the bench in dungarees and a bonnet. A pencil nestled behind one ear and a diamond glass cutter peeped out of a top pocket. Sawdust lay accusingly on his shoulder like undetected dandruff, and small spirals of shavings clung to his clothes, white and clean as babies. After lunch, he walked in carefully, glossy as a rook, wearing a black suit with long black tails like folded wings, a shiny top hat, bow tie, shoes glittering like diamonds, polished to perfection, his cherubic face and red cheeks already practicing the solemn expression befitting his craft.

With usually half an hour to spare, George was in a relaxed mood and, sitting on the sawbench opposite his office, I listened enthralled to his tales of the trade. The District Nurse phoned from a lonely farm up on Benarty Hill.

"I've measured him myself George. He's seven feet two."

"Six feet two, you mean," George replied.

"No, seven feet two," she retorted.

Non-tradesmen were notoriously bad at measuring. Some customers came into the workshop wanting wood or glass saying "It's the length of my elbow to my finger tips plus this bit of string."

George was unwilling to take the Nurse' word for it as he would have to make, or order, a special box. Mounting his bicycle, he cycled the four miles up the hill.

It was dark as he arrived at the farmhouse and knocked at the door . A dog howled somewhere in the gloom. The door swung open suddenly and a gigantic figure stood behind a paraffin lamp.

"Good evening," George whispered, gazing awesomely upwards at the brother of the deceased. George had seen it all, murders, suicides, horrific accidents, and

remained a pleasant, cheerful man, asking nothing out of life or his profession, but an occasional glass of whisky, plug of tobacco and a bet on the 'cuddies' as he called thoroughbred racehorses.

Naturally, I soon became accustomed to the undertaking part of the business and, not wishing to specialize in this, apart from the duties expected from an apprentice, worked away at conventional joiner work on the bench, oblivious to the box on the trestles.

About two years after I started my apprentice-ship, my grandmother died and her coffin, too, lay on the trestles with her name on the shiny plate screwed to the lid. George tactfully poured the pitch in this one himself.

Like most men doing an unpleasant job, George and his assistants reacted by adopting a nonchalant jocularity to their profession. Standard undertaking jokes were repeated often. I heard about the apprentice who went with his master to a house where an old man, who lived alone, had died in bed. His knees had stiffened in a bent position and the apprentice enquired "What will I do?"

"Give them a hard crack with the hammer, son," was the reply .

He complied and the old man suddenly woke, furious.

"What will I do now?" the trembling youth gasped.

"Run for your life, we're in the wrong house."

One old lady had her husband cremated, and his ashes lay in a silver casket on the mantelpiece. A few months, later she lifted the casket for dusting and remarked, "I'm sure Henry is putting on weight," unaware that visitors had been using the casket as an ashtray. Another, more practical, had her husband's ashes installed in an hour glass.

"Aye, Jock widnae work when he wis livin, so I'm makin shair he works noo, see."

On the subject of cremation, I was able to contribute a true story. A relative of my father left instructions in his will that his ashes were to be scattered on the Gairney, his favourite trout burn. He had caught and eaten the fish for years and was returning the compliment. Perhaps he lives on. Every time I see a trout with a slight turn in its eye, usually caused by an earlier fouled hooking, I think of Uncle Samuel.

In the workshop, many tricks were played on apprentices. When first employed they were told to buy a hammer, a footrule and a crosscut saw. Dressed in bib and brace overalls and a new bonnet they strode proudly through the village, hammer slung carelessly in a belt like a Western Colt, miniature journeymen. There was a glamour about being a joiner that other trades didn't seem to possess. Many of us wore collar and ties and shoes rather than boots. After I started working Mother insisted that I polished my own shoes, but despairing of my efforts gave them a very good blacking and polishing one morning. I searched everywhere for my working shoes until Mother finally pointed them out. I could never come up to her expectations of me.

Sometimes the journeymen nailed an apprentice's hammer to the workbench with oval nails, carefully punched in, filled with putty and lightly sanded over. The boy concerned would nearly tear off his nails trying to lift his hammer off the bench. Another trick was to blindfold him and ask if he could split a small block into three equal parts with a hand axe. His brand new checked bonnet would then be substituted for the block and the apprentice would hack vigorously away at his headgear. The apprentice junior to me was forced into a coffin, screwed down, and left for five minutes. Perhaps due to that experience he wasn't attracted to undertaking but became the workshop's expert in Formica , the new plastic just on the market.

One small cock sparrow of a journeyman loved to engage the apprentices in mock boxing matches, hitting them hard, in fun he said. Two of us grabbed him one day, and as he struggled violently at this outrage, slipped, banging his head on the floor, temporarily knocking himself out. He lay still, a fallen cock sparrow, white faced, eyes closed. The other men roared with delight at this diversion.

"You've killed him," one man said happily as he removed the recumbent man's bonnet and placed it on his chest. Another took out his foot rule and measured him up.

A putrid odour seemed to follow me that evening as I left work. I had been dismantling an old stage in the Co-operative Hall and, dirty and dusty, I was glad to get out into the fresh air. The mysterious odour still seemed to be no further away. Putting on my gloves to cycle home, a finger touched something soft and furry. The putrid mouse must have been lying under the stage for weeks and the small journeyman had seized his chance of getting his own back. We fared better than our friends in the pits, however. In time-honoured initiation ceremonies, they were rudely seized, stripped naked and covered with thick black grease. Initiations had a class structure of their own. They varied according to the physical effort or dirtiness of the work. Co-op office boys suffered no greater indignity than to be sent for a 'long stand' or some 'tartan ink.'

Father Flynn was the local Catholic Priest. The best minister in Kelty, George, a Protestant called him. We suspected that this was because George always received a glass of wine when he called at the chapel on business. Father Flynn ordered a new wooden cross for the chapel roof and this was made in the workshop. It was over six feet high although appearing quite small when fixed in position.

I was sent with one of the journeymen to erect the cross and repair sections of the roof. Wull was an excellent tradesman and exceedingly strong. He had the thick waist of the weight-lifter, powerful shoulders, and forearms as thick as my calf muscles.

His three brothers were blacksmiths in the family business and Wull often worked in the smiddy at nights and weekends, usually on the heavy forehammer. We got on very well together but he thought nothing of giving me a clout on the lug if I made a mistake or didn't move quickly enough. That's how he had been treated himself as an apprentice. Like all good tradesmen he was very particular about his tools. Saws were kept in guards, chisels in a special pad and even his hand axe kept in a leather sheath. We fixed the cross in position and stood for a moment holding on to the cross spar enjoying the panoramic view from the chapel roof. Wull could even see the red pantiles of the family smiddy glowing in the sun.

We started to repair a section of the roof next to the cross where a large ventilator had been removed. Below us, a solitary man knelt in prayer. Wull and I sat on the roof one at either side of the gap, attempting to fit a rafter into the main truss.

"Fix your end in first, Jimmy," he cried and I did so, tapping the rafter into a notch with my hammer. Wull gave a sharp tug, my end slipped out, and the heavy rafter swung like a pendulum between his fingers, directly over the man below. Wull needed one hand to hold on to the roof so was forced to hold on to the rafter with one hand only. His mighty forearms bulged and knotted with the strain. I clambered over to help and we pulled the rafter to safety. Far below, the devout old man prayed on, unaware that for several moments the peaceful sanctuary of the chapel had been the most dangerous place in the world for him.

The new cross stood out boldly in the sunlight, its protective shadow falling gently on the seats below. Perhaps George was right and Father Flynn was the best minister in Kelty.

The Priest appeared below and asked in a strong Irish accent "Would you care for a cup of tea now, bhoys?"

We did not confess the incident to him, unsure whether he would classify it as the miracle of St. Joseph's or the Co-op's last job.

CARPENTRY AND CAPERS

Before starting with the Co-operative, I worked for a year with a Glasgow firm on the large housing scheme being built in Kelty. Most of the men were just back from the war and had seen action all over Europe and North Africa. They never spoke about the fighting, mostly relating stories of the seamier side of Egyptian life and the begging ploys of the poor.

"Hi Jock, I'm McGregor from Aberdeen, you buy this nice cloth."

The men came from all over Scotland and some worked on a scheme until it was finished, then moved on to the next, staying in lodgings near the sites. They were trying desperately to pick up the threads of civilian life again but the rough edge of violence was never far from the surface. Some were trainees, men who had served part of their apprenticeship before the war and given a short course afterwards, not always in the same trade but according to demand. Thus an electrician became a joiner and so on. The trainees were often resented by the time-served tradesmen.

Foremen had a difficult task in the circumstances. In my year, two of them were punched on the jaw and the offenders, not waiting to be sacked, strode to the site office for their books. After years of taking orders they seemed to resent any figures of authority. Theft was rampant. It was laughable at closing time to see several men walking stiff-legged off the site with yard-long pieces of flooring tied to their legs inside their overalls. The villagers must have wondered how so many disabled ex-servicemen could be employed on a housing scheme.

Like children, they laughed if you hurt yourself. Once in the winter, I stood on a nail attached to a plank. It pierced my wellington boot and stuck right into my foot. As I hopped round on one leg and with what looked like a large ski on the other, my two journeymen rocked with mirth. One took out his hammer and wrenched out the nail as if he was dismantling a fence. They were a rough a ready bunch, often quick tempered and aggressive but, on the other hand, cheerful and generous. Many of the men gave me small hand tools to build up a kit so that my first tools were stamped with a variety of names. Any gaps in my education were soon rectified, although biology seemed to be the principal subject.

Officially I was an apprentice but I also had to act as 'Nipper,' running messages for the men. At first I was viewed with suspicion. My predecessor had been working a fast one with the bookie's lines. Dicky had evolved a simple scheme. He destroyed several of the lines and pocketed the money. If the horse won he said that he hadn't managed to get the bet on in time and gave the man his stake money back. If it lost, then of course the man concerned was unaware that the bet had not been placed. There were so many men on the site that it was a while before Dicky was suspected. A trap was set, and the bookmaker confirmed that, to his knowledge, Dicky had arrived in time. Like the fly fox he was, he just managed to stay ahead of his pursuers as they chased him from the housing scheme. He was too frightened or wise to return and his books were sent through the post.

One of my tasks was to go round the local shops to collect the quota of cigarettes, then distribute them to the men. The shopkeepers insisted that I bought fifty Pasha, Turkish cigarettes, with every two hundred Capstan or Players. This involved me in a hazardous journey in distribution, many of the men accusing me of keeping the better cigarettes for friends. Surprisingly many of them ordered sweets as they had just come off the ration, and sometimes over a dozen pokes were ordered. I remember once succumbing to temptation, and, taking one sweet from each poke, made up an assortment for myself.

On my rounds of the houses I became very cheeky in response to the rough quips of the men. One joiner became so enraged that he swore violently and chased me out of the house. I laughed over my shoulder as he puffed in pursuit. Suddenly he stopped, and like an Indian brave, drew his hammer from his belt and threw it at my legs, bowling me over. Realising that he had over-reacted, he mumbled a disguised apology, and, seeing that I was only grazed, ambled off. I was wary of Sam after that and made sure he didn't get Pasha too often. Perhaps the Turkish cigarettes affected him in some way. In retrospect, I think that many of the men were slightly disturbed from their war experiences. The men worked in pairs, or mates, and as an apprentice I was sent to work with most of them in turn to experience different types of joiner work such as roofs, floors, partitioning and so on. For a while I was detailed by the foreman to assist two young journeymen from Kirkcaldy who roared into the scheme on a powerful motor bike.

They looked an ill-assorted pair. Jock was tall and gaunt with sad eyes. The other, short, fat and jolly, and unbelievably in this rough squad, was called Cecil. They were both kind and considerate and I loved working with them, but alas, it was not to be for long. Jock drew wickets on the breezeblock wall with a piece of plaster board, while Cecil formed a crude bat. We were laying floors at the time and the windows were still unglazed to allow us to pull up large lengths of flooring.

"Right Jimmy, send them up as fast as you like," Jock shouted, taking up his position at the wall.

I bowled up short cuttings of flooring and he and Cecil took turn about with the bat, trying all sorts of shots, especially through the open windows. We played blissfully for nearly an hour unaware that the flying missiles had been spotted by the Foreman Joiner and the General Foreman. My good companions roared out of my life on their big bike an hour later, only a thin trail of smoke marking their departure and a rough-hewn cricket bat to show that they had ever existed.

An enormous amount of timber was used on the housing scheme and a man was employed full time treating it with creosote. A tall powerful man with the mind of a child, he must have had a surname, but was known to all as Wullie Creosote. Asked one day to burn a large pile of waste paper from glass wool insulation, he stood in the centre, lit the waste, and stood helplessly as the flames licked hungrily at his creosote soaked boiler suit. Two men rushed out, cleared a pathway with long strips of wood and allowed Wullie to escape. The more ignorant of the workmen teased Wullie mercilessly.

The joiners used a soft type of wall boarding composed of compressed paper and wood shavings. This, when sawn, formed a soft mushy waste. As cigarettes were scarce many of the men rolled their own, some by hand, others in a small box with rollers. Using the waste, they rolled Wullie countless cigarettes telling him it was Turkish tobacco. Wullie smoked them all with relish between bouts of creosoting, grateful to have a job in the fresh air instead of risking a bad chest by working underground in the pits.

It is a sad fact of human nature that the strong tend to prey on the weak. Poor Wullie was crucified mentally and physically. One day, two labourers grabbed him, forced him to the wooden floor and nailed him down through the cuffs of his jacket and boiler suit bottoms. Some of the men stood shamefaced but unwilling to intervene.

Wullie was teased and spat on until he went berserk. Tearing his clothes like a savage beast, and breaking from its chains he lifted up the nearest weapon, an axe, and chased his tormentors out of the house. Poor Wullie Creosote, friendly and harmless when treated kindly, but dangerous when taunted. His exploits came to the ears of the foreman and Wullie too departed from the site, perhaps in a way, another casualty of war. His creosote sodden boots left a trail of brown footprints that grew fainter and fainter on the dusty trail to the bus stop.

The firm started another apprentice who took over my 'Nipper' tasks while I. worked permanently at carpentry and joinery. He was a big clumsy, sleepy fellow, always in trouble. One day he failed to return on time with the cigarettes and angry men searched everywhere for him, desperate for a smoke.

"He's a worse nipper than you," Sam said, by way of a compliment, stroking his hammer head menacingly. They were about to give up the search, when, by chance, a joiner opened the door of a broom cupboard, no more than a foot wide and discovered Davy, wedged tightly in, sleeping upright like a horse.

Several years later, Davy and I travelled to Dean Park House in Edinburgh to sit the medical examination for National Service. As the train chugged over the Forth Bridge we vowed to complete the compulsory two years then return to our trade. We met later in the day and Davy informed me that a persuasive Careers Officer had obtained his signature for twelve years service in the Royal Air Force. I used to see him from time to time, a forlorn and forgotten figure, on leave from some foreign station, still looking as if he hadn't slept the night before.

Back (from left)Jock Paterson, Jock Lindsay, Tom Renwick
Front – Jock Fotheringham, Bobby Sneddon

THE DOUGLAS FAMILY

My grandfather was the winding engineman at Lassodie Pit. His photograph shows a man with a heavy black moustache, in collier clothes. Grandfather worked very hard all week, taking on extra shifts and went out one evening a week, usually a Friday, for a drink. He would cycle to Kingseat, two miles away, and get very drunk. At closing time, the barman lifted him on to his bicycle and gave it a push.

Though he couldn't walk steadily, the crouched position on the bike suited him and, aimed in the right direction, he pedalled furiously off. At one notoriously bad bend in the road he would often end up in a ditch and, when he failed to return home, my father would be sent to look for him. He received the routine instructions from Granny to throw a heavy coat over him and bring home his gold watch and chain, the only objects of value left on him after a drinking session. Grandad would stagger home in the early hours of the morning when the cold bit into his drunken slumber.

After heavy drinking he could be very aggressive and terrify his wife and children, even chasing them out of the house, until he fell asleep on the couch. The rest of the week he was a dutiful husband and affectionate father. Grandad died in his mid fifties, worn out with hard work, dust on the lungs and too many nights in damp ditches. I don't know what happened to his gold watch and chain but I have a gold medal that he won for the best gladiolas at Lassodie Flower Show.

My father was born in Lassodie, a small mining village, in 1900. He had three brothers and five sisters and went down the pit at thirteen years old. Because he was small for his age, the gaffer put him in charge of the pit ponies. Though a good scholar, Dad had no option but to go down the pit on leaving school. He was the eldest and extra money was essential.

Two of his brothers followed him in turn, and his sisters started at the pithead, picking stones off the moving belts. His brother Jimmy strayed on to the pit railway track when he was four years old and a train amputated an arm and a leg. A crowd gathered quickly, but no-one could bear to touch the mutilated child, swathed in blood, till his mother arrived, gathered him in her arms without a word, and carried him home. " Dinny worry, Maw," he whispered, " ma arm an leg will grow oan again."

Somehow, he survived and grew up to be a favourite uncle. He would jump over farm gates, swim, play football, and feared nothing or nobody. The ash crutch was more fearsome a weapon than any fist or boot, as many a boy learned to his cost. He often took me fishing as a child, and I watched, fascinated, as he manipulated a worm on to a hook, using his stump better than I could use a hand. Jimmy scorned artificial limbs and pinned up his arm sleeve and trouser leg with big safety pins.

At regular intervals he had to attend hospital after suffering agonies as the bone ends pushed through the flesh at the end of the stumps. No one ever heard him complain. He visited us often and if Mother asked how he was, he would roar out 'Top of the world, Annie' then perform a ritual dance, hopping around on one leg, tossing his crutch in the air and catching it as adroitly as a Drum Major. Jimmy's courage was legendary and he even started a horse drawn fruit and vegetable cart, hopping up and down at every stop to serve customers, sometimes assisted by Grandfather between shifts. Jimmy also studied at the night school and became a recorder at Perth Records Office.

He was popular with the girls, found one who accepted him for what he was, a kind, cheerful, humorous and courageous man, married her and fathered eight children. The last time I saw him he arrived from Perth, twenty miles away on the back of a motor bike, blue with the cold and balancing by superhuman means. "I'm fishing the Gairney today," he grinned cheerfully, and died of a heart attack one month later.

Father's sisters married in turn. Maggie eloped with a visiting boxer from the booths. Nellie married a scrap merchant from Perth who eventually bought Methven Castle. She lived there for several years with her husband and family; quite a change from a small crowded house in Lassodie's miners rows.

As a boy my father roamed the fields and woods surrounding the village collecting wild birds' eggs, snaring rabbits and fishing the burns and ponds. Larks nested in the field close to his house. Placing the young ones in a cage, he moved them a few yards each day until the cage rested on a window sill. In this way the mother lark would feed the young larks until they could fend for themselves, then, transferred inside the house, they sang out their lives, never knowing the soaring ecstasy of the skies. Father acquired two young barn owls, and they were installed in the coal cellar, flying free each night, returning in the early morning to their dark, dusty, domain, ghostly guardians of the black diamonds. Like other boys he used lime sticks to catch linnets, finches and other small birds.

Redpolls were favourite birds with miners and some were trained to pull up their own seed and water in miniature tracks and hutches. Some birds were used as decoys or call birds and they would be placed in a special cage with traps at either end. My father gave me a trap cage in later years and I placed it on a wooden clothes pole in the garden of Braewell.

A flock of redpolls twittered high above and at the sound the redpoll in the cage called out loudly. One left the flock and dropped down to the garden, almost immediately entering the trap cage. They were very trim attractive little birds with distinctive red breasts and heads.

His most unusual pet was a fox cub received from a gamekeeper friend. He tied the fox with a short rope to his border collie, Peg, and the two animals bounded along together, the cub often trying to slip over the dry stane dykes to freedom, but held back by the older, stronger dog. Joe, as he was named, became quite tame and matured into a beautiful, glossy animal, fed daily on rabbits, specially shot for him.

He was kept chained to a wooden peg during the day, in the middle of a hen run of all places, out of reach of strange dogs and teasing children. Joe must have felt like a hungry beggar gazing into a restaurant window. After a few quick fox rushes and the loss of several tail feathers the cackling hens kept their distance.

Joe's bored pacing left a mark in the ground and soon no hen would enter this magic circle, but, strutting nervously about, they carried on with their fowl lives trying to ignore the red deadly intruder. Only the cockerel wanted closer contact to assert his authority in front of his harem but prudence overcame valour, and he contented himself crowing out challenges he hoped would never be accepted. Perhaps due to all the henpecking and other frustrations, Joe turned vicious.

One evening his master put down the plate as usual and nearly lost some fingers as the animal flew at him, clicking its teeth inches away from the outstretched hand, only snatched back in time by the taut chain. Unsentimentally, my father shot the fox, had

him skinned and made into a wrap which his eldest sister proudly wore on Sundays.

So Joe lived on, as it were, curled round a soft white neck, his artificial glassy eyes gazing at the hills he had never quite reached.

THE JONES FAMILY

Mother also came from a large family. Her mother bore twelve children, losing two of them shortly after birth. She was the youngest girl and the second youngest in the family. Her father was known locally as 'The Wee Welshman,' and was considered eccentric. He dressed in unusual clothes, wore a cheese-cutter hat and golden earrings. In his wedding photograph, he has a white suit, a black moustache and a sardonic air. Grandad Jones originally came from Liverpool, ran away from an unhappy home at ten years old and arrived at Wales, where he lived for several years.

He worked all over Britain and eventually came to Inverkeithing, getting a labouring job on the construction of the Forth Railway Bridge. Grandmother Jones too, had an unhappy childhood, brought up by a stepmother. She left home as soon as possible and went into service in Inverkeithing. Her future husband was a lodger in the house next door and she was rather frightened by the older dark, Spanish looking workman but flattered by his obvious interest. She had only walked out with him several times when he asked her to be a witness at a friend's wedding in a registry office. Grandmother hesitated, then agreed. They met the other couple at the office and the Registrar started to write down details, asking her what seemed to be unnecessary questions considering she was only a witness. Becoming suspicious, she demanded an explanation.

"You and I are to be married, Nell," my grandfather said wistfully.

"What! Marry a funny little Spaniard like you? Never." she cried.

He tried to coax her into matrimony, and the wedding was suspended while it gradually dawned on her that, in all the wide world, here was the first person who seemed to care whether she lived or died. Seeing her hesitation, he fumbled nervously in an inner jacket pocket, probably for the ring. Grandmother, in her bewilderment, thought he was drawing a knife to add to his persuasions, so piratical was Grandfather's appearance. She quickly consented, they returned to the bemused registrar and completed the formalities. Grandmother followed her husband as he tired of one job and searched for another. They arrived back in Wales, where she bore her first two children. They eventually came to Kelty and shortly afterwards Grandmother received a small legacy and bought Braewell Cottage. She refused to accompany her husband on his travels again.

"Twelve sideboards in twelve years is enough for any woman, Harry," she told him.

Of their large family, the eldest went to seek his fortune in America. Two of the sons went to live in Wales, perhaps lured by their father's romantic reminiscences. In Cefn Fforest, one started a grocer's shop and the other a barber's. Their youngest son, Jimmy, was killed in France in 1914 aged eighteen, without ever having a single leave home. Granny took to bed on receiving the telegram and never really recovered from the shock. One son tried the pit for a day then volunteered for the army the next. Such were the options in a mining village.

Grandfather could never settle in one place for long and left home at regular intervals, looking for work, or avoiding it some said. He was a natural wanderer and did this until he was too old and arthritic to take to the road. An old lady who knew him well delighted in telling me that my Grandfather left Braewell one morning to get a can filled with paraffin for the lamp. It was a lovely day, the sky was blue and the blackies whistled in the hawthorn hedge. The open road beckoned. He hid the can under the hedge and returned a week later with the can full, as if he had only been away an hour or so.

By the time my mother was about eight years old, Grandfather was becoming more and more confined to Braewell Cottage. He must have resembled my father's pet fox, longing for freedom, surrounded by cackling hens of women and would viciously nip any arm or leg coming too close to his sagging imprisoning armchair.

Like many of the young women in the village, Mother went into service on leaving school, working in several farmhouses and once in a manse. For a while, she was employed in a farm at Kingsbarns near St. Andrews, where the fields ran down to a lovely, lonely beach,. The work was hard but she enjoyed it there. Up at six in the morning to milk the cows, she then scrubbed and polished all day until six in the evening. Later on in the evening, the mistress would often hand her darning.

"In case you get bored," she said .

It must have been little better than slavery. She got one day off a week and cycled home to Kelty, a distance of over thirty miles. Like her sisters, all her meagre wages were handed over to her mother, receiving only a small pittance back as pocket money. After a few hours at Braewell it was time to cycle the long journey back.

Mother also worked in the Cottage Hospital, Pittenweem and the Matron there appointed her hospital cook at seventeen years of age, so efficient were the young women of the time. I visited the Matron, still in charge of the hospital in 1955, twenty five years after my Mother left.

She told me "I only had one complaint about Annie's cooking. This was from a big burly young man who was always slightly aggressive. I told him to go down to the kitchen and ask for the cook. She was pointed out, a slight girl of seventeen barely five feet tall. He left the kitchen without a word."

When Grandmother took ill, my Mother returned to Kelty and took a job at the pithead of the Lindsay Colliery. A happy girl by nature she sang as she worked, picking stones from the moving belt. Her dour gaffer warned her several times to stop as she distracted the other girls from their work and too many stones were being allowed to slip through. Mother kept forgetting her warnings and finally, his patience exhausted, he gave her the sack halfway through "Ae fond kiss and then we sever."

She then obtained a job as a barmaid at the Gothenburg Public House, where she met my father, who was attracted to this small smiling girl, the only barmaid he had known who kept telling many of the customers that they had consumed enough drink for one evening. This didn't please the manager, of course, and her career was in jeopardy. Father had arrived at an opportune time in her life.

They got married quietly soon after they met. My uncle, the scrap merchant, lent them his car, the only one in the whole of the family, for the day.

"I know you've never driven a car before, John," he said, " but there's nothing to it. That's the brake, that's the clutch, there's the throttle. Now away you go and have a nice day."

Uncle shook hands with both of them and off they meandered to Kingsbarns, Father not sure what was going to be the hardest to control, the strange car or the determined young woman by his side. Their total assets after their wedding were twenty pounds and Mother promptly bought four watercolours at two pounds each even though they had very little furniture. Returning the car at night, they set up house with my grandmother, now widowed, at Braewell Cottage. At the time, my father was employed as a stripper, one of the hardest jobs in mining at the Lindsay Colliery. Shortly after I was born he was working at the coal face when the roof caved in on him.

In a roar of dust and debris a large boulder pinned him to the ground, fracturing one leg in six places. His mates attempted to rescue him immediately but twice they had to withdraw as the roof creaked and groaned and stones kept thudding down. Father, fully conscious, had to wait half an hour before he was rescued, thinking every moment his last. He was off work for four years and we lived on parish relief. Some of the fractures refused to heal and his plaster of paris casts had to be changed several times, eventually leaving him with a permanent limp.

Braewell Cottage was rather damp. There was supposed to be a well in the vicinity which may have accounted for this. The cottage was well situated though, standing high with steep steps leading to the front door. The back garden led down to the Black Burn, marking the boundary between Fife and Kinross. Lying warm and snug in bed at night, you could hear the sound of the water, usually soothing, sometimes angry and hissing in spate, the trees sighing in the wind, twigs tap-tapping at the window as if seeking shelter.

Since the cottage was high, the views on a good day were wide and varied. At the back of the house, Benarty dominated the vista, guarding the sparkling waters of Loch Leven. To its right, other hills, triangular as the pyramids of Egypt, black and forbidding - the slag tips of the Fife Collieries. The land surrounding them looked ravaged, bleak and desolate, sparse grass and stunted trees.

The water from the pits was pumped into a depression known as 'The Meedies,' originally meadows. This large stretch of water was surrounded by miniature tips of slag and a lonely single track railway stretched a long finger across to Lochore. Near our house, a sign read, 'Warning. This part of the road is liable to subsidence.' This frightened and puzzled me. Were you supposed to run over the spot quickly or tiptoe softly, one foot at a time in case a chasm suddenly appeared and you could pause on the brink of, perhaps, Hell itself. I knew it was down there some where. I had overheard the old miners saying that it was Hell underground in the Lindsay Pit.

From the front of Braewell Cottage the scene changed dramatically. Low wooded hills and dense forests of spruce and larch owned by the Forestry Commission. To the right lay Blairadam Estate built up by William Adam, the classical architect. The big house could be seen surrounded by trees, parks, walled gardens and streams. On the estate was Kiery Craigs Lodge where Sir Walter Scott wrote part of his novel *The Abbot*. This then was Kelty. On the border of the Fife coalfields but surrounded by glorious countryside, a warm and friendly community.

"Aye laddie, ah ken yir faither and ah mind o yir grandfaither. Yir uncle hid a horse and cairt at wan time. Yir mither's faither wis a funny wee man wi gold earrings, ye ken, and yir granny had a wee shop a the fit o the brae. She sellt hame made potted heid and treacle toffee."

One old lady capped them all.

"Whit's yer name son? Oh that's wha ye are. As saw ye before yir mither did, and a richt skinny wee thing ye wir, tae. Tell her Nurse Hayne's is askin for her."

The village was divided into three main types of houses; privately owned, Coal Board and Council. It had two picture houses, seven pubs, two churches, one chapel, one hotel, a play park, tennis courts and about five thousand inhabitants; always some underground night and day.

Jackie lived across the street, Pud next door and children of all ages swarmed the streets before affluence brought the perils of the motor car.

Mother with Lucky

THE PITS

Dark is the night from whence I came,
black as the pit from pole to pole,
I thank whatever Gods may be
for my unconquerable soul.

So wrote the poet and unwittingly gave an apt description of miners. Unconquerable men they were, strong and gentle, comrades in adversity, good husbands and fathers, humorists in appalling conditions. Above all, they shared the common bond of men working in dangerous places. No conscripts were needed to rescue trapped mates, the volunteers were there, ready and willing. Every miner had the blue scars left where coal dust entered cuts.

Each man donated three pence of his pay, a penny each for the brass band and the pipe band and a penny for the children's Gala Day. Gambling schools could be seen in bits of waste ground, small fortunes to be made on the landing of two coins – 'a pound ah heed thum.' Warm, generous to a fault, they gambled on horses, cards and whippets, as they gambled daily with their lives. One young miner with a wife and two young children lost all his wages at a tossing school. The rest of the men, ever generous, took a collection for him and made up most of his wages.

Tam, stricken with the gambling fever, wanted to start again, but the men chased him angrily away. The gaffers kept well away from the gambling schools and wisely so. Any figure in authority was the rock on which they broke their waves of wrath, a built-in safety device, a recognisable object on which to transfer some of the fear and frustrations of their lives. A noted gaffer with a prominent lower lip made a condescending remark about one of his men.

"Oh he's a fine lookin lad, a pity though he his that turn in his ee."

The recipient got to hear about this and tackled the gaffer on the subject.

"Whit ir you talkin aboot? Ye've as much slack lip hingin there that wid tak twa dugs aw their time tae drag intae a close."

Few miners swore in their own homes, however bad the language used at work. Swearing was another safety valve in dangerous situations, but their homes were sanctuaries, and high standards of speech and behaviour expected of their children. I never once heard my Father swearing in the house, yet he wakened Mother sometimes during the night with loud oaths as he re-lived his accident and other nightmarish situations.

Miners were humble, modest, men. Before the introduction of pithead baths, the miners bathed at home in great zinc tubs in front of the fire, filled with hot water from large black kettles or pots. Children were chased out of the room while their father washed.

Some of the older men still refused to have the coal dust scrubbed from their backs, telling their wives that this weakened them. A miner with a weak back was finished.

Their clothes were filthy with coal dust and wives had a difficult time trying to turn out their husbands for the following shift.

Miners' pleasures were simple - gambling, fishing, dugs, pubs, doos and football. Most of them drank, washing down the dust with pints of beer; few drank to excess. Apart from the cost, a man doing hard brutal work had to be very fit. Unfortunately, most miners smoked, as this only aggravated their chest conditions. Apart from the pools, horses, tossing schools and dogs, they would gamble on anything. Who could jump the longest or highest or drink the most beer in one gulp. Dog racing was very popular and men could always be seen in the village exercising their whippets, thin ugly dogs, some with a tendency to bite and wearing muzzles.

Many tricks were played on newcomers to the pits. During the second world war, Bevin Boys, men conscripted to work in the mines, trained at Muircockhall , near Dunfermline and some were detailed to Kelty pits. At Benarty mine, some miners who were keen fishermen, smuggled in a pail full of trout caught in Loch Leven   and poured them into a pool down the pit. On being shown around, the Bevin Boys were astonished to see trout leaping out of the water.

"Aye, we must be getting too near to the loch," one of the miners remarked.

In a mining village, pits were never far from our thoughts. The black pyramids loomed large on the horizon and the constant accidents reminded everyone that they could be the next to lose a father, son, brother or husband. There were too many widows and fatherless children in the village to allow us to forget the cost in human lives of extracting coal from a reluctant earth.

Some of the West Fife Pits were called after the wives and daughters of the coal owners.Thus we had the *Mary, Dora* and the *Jenny Gray.* In spite of such euphoric titles the reality of each was similar with various degrees of bad roofs, low runs, black damp and water. They were all dusty, dirty, seductive maidens promising more money for extra shifts while ignoring the perils in their hot clammy embrace.

A pit near Kelty was called the Peeweep. Yes, larks and peewits trilled their lovely haunting melodies in the fresh air of the fields around the shaft while far below them canaries sang no more as they toppled in their cages, often the first sign the miner had that gas was present. Under the village was a vast labyrinth of tunnels, a gigantic human warren that made houses above cant slightly to one side, depressions to appear in the fields and roads to crack ominously in places.

In the fields were breathing holes, shafts built with bricks, dangerous places where a blackbird nesting on a ledge could lure a foolhardy boy. In the relentless search for coal some of the runs became very close to the surface. In Benarty mine a falling roof revealed a blue sky and white clouds above. At Cowdenbeath, miners emerged into the middle of a hen run, blinking their eyes at the strong light, the hens squawking and fluttering at this intrusion into their ordered lives. For a while the men came up to the surface **to** eat their piece and the hens started to look forward to their visit as they were fed on scraps by the black denizens of another world, not like pink and polished Mrs. Muir at all who normally fed them.

Cheese was the thing for sandwiches; it kept the best. Underground, rats scuttled over miners' legs, searching for food at piece time, and black flies settled on their pieces like locusts. One grizzled old miner who worked with my father refused to brush them off. "There's nothin like a bit o fresh meat," he said philosophically.

Our meat, like everything else, came from the Co-operative Society, which along with the pit, seemed to dominate our lives. The Co-op had shops everywhere, Bakers, Butchers, Fishmongers, Drapery, Grocery, and a large Building Department. Everyone had a check number. 1271 was imprinted on our minds to be given immediately when asked by Co-op employees. The women looked forward to the dividend every year. This enabled them to buy necessary clothes and shoes for the children. It was a form of saving, most women being unable to bank any money. The word 'divi' became a magical word to the children, like Christmas or Gala-day

"You'll get yir new troosers when the divi comes."

The Co-op sufficed all our needs. We were always being sent for messages, a pound of sugar, matches, and best of all, new bread. We would clutch a new loaf, still warm and steaming from the ovens, with a dark crust, and peel off large strips to eat on the way home. The Society also had vans and horse drawn carts. The horses knew the rounds as well as the vanmen and would stop automatically at certain gates, where the housewives very often gave them a piece.

The milk horse stopped regularly at our gate and deposited dung as a matter of course. As soon as it moved on, Mother would ask one of us to go out with the shovel and pail to collect the deposits, or as she called them *horses d'oeuvres*, for the roses.

We were very reluctant to do this. Pals were always ready to shout disparaging remarks and Mother would usually end up lifting the dung herself. Henry's wife, Jean collected the baker's horse dung every day, claiming ownership as part of her dividend. She was outraged once when a new English tenant across the street rushed out and secured the prized particles for herself.

"Did ye see that besom jist noo?" she complained to a neighbour, "and she's no even a member."

It must have been grand stuff. Father grew the best roses in the street, at least the ones Pud allowed to reach maturity.

In the Winter, the roads became very slippery, made worse by the slides the children made and the horses had great difficulty keeping their balance. The vanmen became irritable and bad tempered. The milk horse, as usual, stopped at our gate and straddled a long slide. We became very daring, sliding down to the horse and jumping off at the last minute. Pud, clumsy as ever, slid right under the horse's belly and crouched shivering with cold and fright, too petrified to move, blinking like a fledgling bird. The milkman dragged him out by the collar cursing him for frightening his horse.

The Clydesdales were really lovely big animals, usually very gentle. Father would sometimes send me down to the stables with a bag to collect hay seed and from this he produced lovely lawns. I loved the warm earthy smell of the stables though the passage behind the horses seemed too narrow as they nervously shuffled their enormous legs. It was amazing how the vanmen dominated these giants. One small man would slap and shove a horse about shouting, "Get ower a bit, Star," and the the big horse would move reluctantly but obediently, treating him as a minor irritation, like a horse fly. A job with the Co-op was the acme of ambition. "Get a job there and that's you set fir life," parents would say. Now the pits and the Co-op have all gone.

The Bevin Boys

Nivver mind. It could have been a pigsty

PUD, JACKIE AND CRAW

Pud was a bully. He was destined for obesity in later years but at fourteen his fatness gave extra weight to his fists, and he hammered younger boys whenever the chance arose. Pud had what we called a *Baw heid*, the skull large and bumpy, the fair hair kept closely cropped which seemed to accentuate the contours. Small bald patches proclaimed, like medals, battles lost or won. His trunk-like legs seemed to be bursting out of his short trousers and his elbows jutted out of his jersey like rocks emerging from the sea. His hands and knees acted as hosts to crops of warts.

Pud only seemed to smile when someone else was hurt and most of the time he assumed a sullen scowl. At a safe distance some of his younger victims would chant, "All of a sudden a big mealy pudden came flying through the air."

Pud, though strong, was no runner, but he had a great memory. He nursed his wrath, like Tam o Shanter's wife, to keep it warm until an opportunity arose to get his own back. Pud had a great memory. Only a mother could love him, and she did, with all the fierce protective instinct of the female tigress. His father had volunteered for the army shortly before the war began and was now a sergeant in the Black Watch. Pud's mother transferred all her loyalty and affection to her one offspring.

After Pud set fire to Farmer McKenzie's haystack, a policeman called at the house and left five minutes later convinced that he had set fire to the haystack himself and should be fighting at the front, not amusing himself annoying poor servicemen's wives and children at home. Soon after the war started an evacuee arrived in a car to stay with Pud's mother for the duration of the war; he may have been a relative. After a few days, Pud attempted to punch and kick Thomas whenever he thought his mother wasn't looking. Thomas hadn't lived in Glasgow for nothing, though, and gave as good as he got. Pud resented this cuckoo planted in his nest but, after a while, they formed an uneasy truce and in a way he began to look on the younger boy as an adopted brother.

Pud had a special interest in our garden which my father, like many miners, was very fond of. He cultivated peas, strawberries, turnips and other fruits and vegetables. Pud knew exactly when each was ready for eating, and I suspect that he inspected the crops each night to check progress. If he had just eaten his fill it wouldn't have been so bad but he often destroyed more than he consumed in wanton fits of destruction, much like a stoat entering a hen house. His mother, of course, refused to believe anything against her son until my father kept watch one night and saw Pud climbing out of his bedroom window in pyjamas, then entering our garden like a jealous landowner inspecting his estate by moonlight. She did put a stop to his nocturnal wanderings after that, but Pud had many tricks.

Stones were flung in our doorway and once my mother went to her washing line and found three sets of scarce nylon stockings held by pegs, with the feet neatly snipped off. They looked most peculiar when she carried them in, the first time we had seen nylon ankle socks. This wasn't as bad, though, as the fright Miss Knight, a middle-aged spinster received. She lived next door to Arthur Erskine, an odd character and was horrified to discover that Arthur had attached a pair of his heavy woollen socks to her suspender belt on the communal drying green as there was no empty spaces left. At least, that was his explanation.

Pud's father came home on leave once and brought him an air pistol. Pud promptly walked down the field beside the Black Burn. There was a small, square brick tank filled with water, something to do with the sewage. Half a dozen frogs had found it an ideal place to lay their spawn and Pud had noticed them the night before. He shot each one in turn as it rose to the surface for air. His mother wisely threw the pistol in the Black Burn after her husband departed.

Pud kept a pigeon as a pet and searching in the desert of his nature, found a small oasis of affection for the bird. It fluttered above his head and shoulder while he fed it on scraps of bread soaked in milk, muttering to it 'Pees, pod, pod, pod' or similar doo endearments.

'Oh gin ah were a doo, I'd flee awa the noo,' my Mother used to say in her more harassed moments, but Pud's doo had no intention of leaving this source of food and attention. Pud was a curious mixture. He loved this scrawny doo but set mousetraps for starlings. Those bold, swaggering buccaneers of birds would fly down and snatch so quickly at a lump of cheese that the trap would usually miss them and they would fly off in alarm at the sudden snap, squawking in fear.

Occasionally, the trap would catch one by the lower mandible, breaking it and the poor bird could be seen for days afterwards, the bottom part of its beak hanging like a drooping gate, condemned to slow starvation.

My father had used part of an old dresser to construct a garden fence. The wood was about one inch thick and the ornamental top resembled a switchback railway with humps and hollows. Jackie and I collected caterpillars from the cabbages and had great fun racing them along the track. The green ones were fairly slow, then we found two hairy black caterpillars. They moved along at an astonishing rate, humping and stretching, not inclined to stray off the course.

"I've got one that can beat yours," shouted Pud, arriving with his faithful doo on his shoulder. We bet a penny each on our protegés and gave my young sister the money to hold for the winner. Pud's caterpillar certainly was impressive, hairy, but coloured a reddish brown and larger than its two opponents. Off they went at a grub gallop on the yard long race, a cabbage leaf placed enticingly at the winning post.

Pud's led most of the way, then suddenly stopped six inches from the finish, I suppose out of puff. Mine had turned round and was galloping back to the start. Jackie's, the slowest, reached the end of the course, crawling gratefully onto the cabbage leaf. Pud, never gracious in defeat, squashed his own with a warty fist and lumbered off in the huff. He joined us with the evacuee after tea and we walked beside the Black Burn to a field near McKenzie's farm. The corn was about three feet high and we had a marvellous time, wrestling, pushing, rolling about, flattening large patches of the crop. Pud was enjoying himself, not being too rough in case the three of us joined forces against him. Suddenly, the farmer bore down on us like a wild bull, his two pronged fork held in front. We rushed for a hole in the hedge and I made it to safety with Thomas and Jackie.

Pud, the slowest and fattest, jammed in the hedge and McKenzie gave him a sharp prod in the buttocks. Pud came scrambling down the hill roaring like a lost calf, his pride and person rudely punctured. McKenzie had exacted his revenge for his burned haystack.

Jackie had fair, curly hair, blue eyes that blinked often, strong limbs and was accident prone. His hands and knees were criss-crossed with scars like a map of mishaps and he wore sticking plaster as the girls wore rings and bangles.

Guddling for trout, he was adept at finding a broken bottle or a rusty tin to stand on. Even sitting still, blinking his wide blue eyes and sniffing nervously like a rabbit, he attracted trouble. At the Miners' Welfare Boys Club, the leader formed a square with four P.E. benches. Jackie sat down to watch the boxing. A big lad threw a punch, his smaller opponent ducked and Jackie got it right on the nose.

In later years, he started as an apprentice bricklayer. Dismantling a chimney in a house to be renovated, Jackie formed part of a chain passing bricks from man to man. He was the first link on the ground.

"How's Jackie?" a friend shouted from the road. He turned his head and the brick he was supposed to catch nearly split his head in two. He was driven to hospital and returned later with close-cropped hair and several stitches in a great horseshoe scar. A month later, climbing into an attic through a hatch, he took hold of a worn electric wire. Hearing the screams, his journeyman rushed to the spot to see two violently kicking legs. He switched off the mains and Jackie dropped to the floor, tingling all over.

The youngest of a family of five boys, he was always glad to escape from the bustle of an overcrowded home to roam the hills and field. My best friend Jackie, sniffing, blinking, companion in countless escapades, an adventurer, never climbed the tall trees for rooks nests though, thinking with his luck he could never survive such a fall.

I remember the day Thomas arrived at Pud's. A big black car stopped and a tall thin man in a dark suit got out carrying a briefcase. A small boy then emerged carefully in a new brown suit and black leather boots, with the cardboard box containing his gas mask hanging from a string round his neck.

He sniffed the air cautiously "What's that funny smell?"

"Fresh air son, you're not in Glasgow now, you know."

Pud's mother wasn't a bad sort really. She welcomed Thomas into her home but let him know that Pud was number one in the house and Thomas was expected to do most of the chores; bring in the coal, weed the garden, what little was cultivated, and generally ensure that her son wasn't bothered too much with menial tasks. After all, Pud had his doo to feed. The evacuee was such an engaging character that I'm sure she grew fond of him eventually.

In Kelty, anyone called Crawford was known as Craw, so the boy from Glasgow was known as Thomas for a short while only then became Craw like the rest of the clan. He was a small square tough boy, friendly and generous, with the courage of a lion. His yellow hair stuck out in spikes above a boxer's face with flattened nose and freckles.

No boy was too big for Craw to fight, no tree too tall to climb and no girl too ugly to kiss. With all the resourcefulness and worldly knowledge of the city boy, he became the leader of our small group, mostly consisting of Jackie and me. We roamed the countryside in search of adventure during the school holidays as wild and free as the creatures we encountered. Only one subject was taboo, Craw's previous life in Glasgow. After being rudely snubbed a few times, Jackie and I never referred to it again.

"There's a peewit rising," Jackie shouted one day. He stood still, fixing his eyes on the spot. Craw and I walked forward to his direction

"A bit to the left, a wee bit more, straight on, about there."

The two eggs lay in a slight hollow, barely a nest at all. Overhead the female peewit was crying frantically, swooping down so low we could feel the draught of her wings. Jackie came running up triumphantly.

"Ah kent it wis a nest," he shouted.

We agreed that Craw should take one and leave the other alone. We watched, dumbfounded, as he punched a hole in the pointed end with his penknife and drained the raw contents with obvious relish, keeping the shell as the first egg of a collection. This act confirmed his leadership. Any boy who could drink raw eggs was surely worth following. No other boy we knew had done this. Craw quickly acquired the finest collection of eggs in the street. Later we discovered that he had painted many of the 'rare' species himself with amazing varieties of spots and squiggles. No wonder we could not match this colourful imp.

We stole quietly past the big house at Blairadam. The Captain was alright if you asked permission to walk through the estate but adventurers didn't ask permission. The rooks cawed noisily in the tall trees, making such a clamour that we became uneasy. Something glittered in a window of the Big House, then winked several times like an evil eye in the glow of the sun.

"Let's run. That will be the Captain with his binoculars," Jackie whispered. We ploughed through the leaves, leaving deep furrows and causing the rooks to rise from their nests, clamouring louder than ever. We ran until we were well clear of the estate and flopped down at Dichendad where a spring bubbled from the ground to form a pool in a stone trough. This spot was famous for its magical properties and the spring, known locally as The Iron Water, stained the stones and ground surrounding a dark rusty red.

We lay face downward, heads touching and drank like animals, noisily sucking the water, a lovely cool drink with a slight tang of metal. Climbing over a fence we entered the 'Doo Wids,' one of our special haunts, a mixture of spruce, larch and pine with the occasional oak and beech. In the heart of the woods it was as quiet as a cathedral. We stood on a thick carpet of needles talking in whispers. The light filtered through the trees forming pools of sunlight occasionally at a bare patch. Sometimes we had to crawl on our hands and knees to avoid the low branches.

On a previous outing I disturbed a large hornet which flew straight at me and stung me on the forehead. We came to a fallen tree and sat down for a while, grateful for the respite. Here we were cut off from the world in our private cocoon. No grimfaced teachers, giggling girls, boring chores or black slag tips. This was a domain for boys, too low for men, too tough for girls. We belonged here, with the fox and the rabbit, the grey squirrel and the stoat.

"We smoke peace pipe," Craw said solemnly, taking a puff of a cigarette end then passing it round. We were red men, hunters of the primeval forest. We didn't have to paint our faces, the trees camouflaged us in their own way. Pine needles stuck in our hair like feathers, our faces were criss-crossed in fine dark lines by the low branches and our hands a deep red, sticky from the resin of the trunks. The woods embraced us, whispered softly in our ears 'Leave the coal towns, dwell here forever, you're already half savage, stay the night and you'll be boys no more.'

"Hi, leave me a puff," Craw grumbled noisily

As its name suggests, the wood was a haven for wood pigeons or, as we called them, cushy doos. Their low soothing murmur was the flute section of the wood orchestra while the sudden loud clapping of wings, the percussion, made us jump in alarm. Their nests were easily seen from the ground, a few sparse twigs with occasionally the round, white eggs shining through.

We acquired a lot of knowledge in the Doo Wids. There were so many nests built over the years that we had to know these in current use. Usually several small, white fluffy feathers lay on the ground underneath, and the nest, even from below, had a lived-in look, like an occupied house. Tiny pellets, broken apart to reveal small bones and fur told us that a tawny owl was in possession and the tree had to be climbed with caution.

Before Craw acquired our wood lore, he made a dramatic blunder. He climbed up a tall larch, no longer Hawkeye but Tarzan of the Apes and his loud yodelling call, the echoes making the doos suddenly quiet, told us he had reached the nest. Finding a single egg, he popped it into his mouth to allow his hands free for climbing. He fell suddenly as a branch snapped and he came down like a falling star, the mattress of leaves breaking his fall.

A hideous odour assailed our nostrils as Craw danced about spitting like a snake. In between choicest Glasgow swear words we gathered that the nest had lain deserted for weeks and the egg was putrid. A lot of cushy doos were shot, even in the nesting season, being considered vermin by the farmers, and it was not unusual to find cold eggs and dead young doos.

Not wishing to pass the Captain and his binoculars again, we took another route back, nearer the pits. A barn owl flew out from a deep depression in the ground. This was part of a disused pit, and dangerous with crumbling steep slopes leading to a dark pool with iron girders sticking out like broken, rotten teeth from a witch's mouth.

Climbing down carefully, we discovered an old fireclay drain about a foot in diameter with a warm musty smell suggesting a nest. Peering into the darkness, we observed three owlets with heart shaped faces and startled expressions. An addled egg lay among the remains of countless small rodents forming a furry bony floor.

"Gimme that long bit o wire beside ye," I whispered to Jackie "Ah'll try and git wan oot fir a pet."

I formed a shape like a shepherd's crook and poked the wire into the drain. The owlets retreated further back into the gloom, clucking their beaks in fright or anger until only the three white masks glowed feebly, well out of reach. The egg was easily rolled out and Craw claimed it for his collection. A swirling movement in the pool caught our attention.

We climbed down and witnessed an astonishing spectacle. Someone had drowned a dog, a whippet by the look of it, in a potato sack, weighed with stones. The hessian had deteriorated and the corpse exposed. Hundreds of tadpoles were feasting on the decaying flesh.

"They're monsters," Jackie gasped in astonishment.

"Aye, wan of them wid tak yir fit aff," Craw exclaimed.

The abundance of meat had indeed changed the tadpoles' natural growth and they were an inch and a half in length with heads like marbles. There were no signs of legs appearing as would be expected from some at least and they bore little resemblance to the merry little fellows we kept in jam jars, but seemed to stare at us with beady unblinking eyes.

I dreamt of them that night nibbling at my flesh as they had nibbled at the whippet and woke screaming to be comforted by mother. We never returned to find out if the giant tadpoles grew into giant frogs.

"Ah'll tell Pud some wan hid a sack o coins in this pool," Craw grinned "There's mair fat on him than a whippet fir the tadpoles."

Climbing out of the pit, we discovered a young barn owl fast asleep on the low branch of a tree, perhaps the first young one to leave the nest or more probably one of the first brood, as it looked nearly mature. It was one of the most beautiful things I had ever seen, golden speckled cape with white face and under parts, still as a statue, almost within reach.

Jackie volunteered his shirt to throw over the owl if Craw and I did the climbing, and to look out for the mother if it came to the defence of its offspring. We climbed up the tree as quietly as possible, the slightest breaking of a twig sounding amplified and surely the bird could hear the pounding of our hearts. Jackie shivered below, his chattering teeth adding to the cacophony.

The owl slept on, only a slight movement of its head showing that it was alive. Craw and I didn t want to get too close, the talons and beak looked formidable weapons. We stood on a thick branch below the owl, the shirt between us, holding a sleeve each. Craw nodded and we threw the shirt like a net.

The effect was sudden and dramatic, the owl flew from under the canopy with a terrifying screech, straight at my face, only one talon caught in the cloth. I fell backwards and landed on Jackie, his eyes blinking rapidly upwards in alarm. The bird flapped clumsily over the pit we had recently climbed out of, the shirt billowing behind it for an instant, then dropped into the dark pool below.

Jackie looked enquiringly at Craw. "Ah'm frozen, will ye git ma shirt back fir me?"

Craw was brave, Craw was the best climber, Craw was our leader, but dusk was falling and no way was Craw going to wade barefooted in among those giant tadpoles.

"A'll gie ye a shirt jist like the wan ye had," he said grandly, "Race ye baith hame."

DOGS

Jealousy was Henry's trouble, a gripping, all embracing jealousy that soured his nature and made him a bit of an outcast in a small, close community. He ate his piece alone at the pit, avoiding the other men, a bad thing when your life often depended on your mates. He was a small man with close cropped grey hair and even his eyes weren't neighbours, one blue, the other brown. His wife Jean was a large fat woman with a faded beauty.

To Henry, though, she was a prized jewel, waiting to be snatched by an amorous thief. No male could enter his house, even the rent man, a potential threat, conducted his business on the front door step where he could be chaperoned by inquisitive neighbours in Henry's absence.

A rag and bone man came round the village regularly with his horse and cart. Like other traders he had his own peculiar cry 'Eeeeaye,' enough to send the children surging to their mother for rags. A small bundle won a balloon and a large one a goldfish.

Jean was weeding her garden when he stopped at the gate, a dark gypsy looking man with white teeth and black curly hair. "C'mon lady, bring me a bundle of rags and I'll give you the finest goldfish you've ever seen." He held it up in a jar for inspection.

"Oh I've a better looking one than that in the house," she laughed, "I'll prove it to you, and you can have some rags for nothing."

Henry was watching from behind the curtains. When his wife returned with her goldfish, Henry snatched the fish out of the bowl and threw it on the fire. When Jean complained to a neighbour, she said "Oh what a shame. He might have drowned it."

Henry drank. He went every Saturday night to the Gothenburg and drank steadily and morosely in a corner. Returning home he kicked furiously at doors, all his frustrations coming to boiling point. Jean kept out of the way until he quietened down, not that she was frightened of him, because one swipe of her big hand could have knocked Henry flat.

She was fond of him in her own way, perhaps flattered that he considered her such a prized possession. They had no children, so in a way Jean treated her diminutive spouse like a boy.

"Noo, noo, it's no as bad as that, gie's a tune on the fiddle."

So Henry played the fiddle to her, jigs, reels and the haunting Londonderry Air keeping all the neighbours awake until the early hours of Sunday morning. Henry was Jean's second husband. She had lost her first man in a pit accident and never was a husband so truly lost, for not the slightest trace of him remained in the house to show that he had ever existed. Henry made sure of that. All his possessions were jealously guarded. He had the finest garden in the street, treating slugs and snails much the way he treated other men, interlopers in his domain. Every plant was tended and nurtured to perfection, even Pud never ventured near this garden.

Henry had a dog. Trixie wasn't much of a dog as dogs go, small, black, protruding eyes and inclined to slaver, but she was Henry's dog and she shared, equally with Jean, his affection. No male dogs ventured near their gate. Henry had some sort of spray that he used often and vigorously on the posts. Henry looked on boys with suspicion; they were miniature men, weren't they, but Jean had a soft spot for them. The evacuee, especially, brought out her mother instinct, and she was from Glasgow originally herself.

Craw adored dogs. He had not been allowed pets in the city tenements and Pud's mother, house-proud, wouldn't consider one either. He pleaded with Jean to be allowed to take Trixie for a walk. He would be very careful. At last she gave in. Craw could be very persuasive.

"But mind and be back before he gets hame from the backshift or he'll shoot me."

Trixie was in her element. "Rats, Fetchit, Seestum," such marvellous words, heard only at a distance before.

Jackie and I joined them, and we walked along one of the Forestry Commission tracks. Trixie chased a rabbit and we followed her into the dense Norwegian spruce. We were near the trapper's cottage by now and crept past stealthily, the black dog leading the three of us like Indians in single file to avoid too much snapping of twigs. Trixie, still sniffing the ground, entered a clearing, there was a sudden snap and a yelp, and a gin trap held her by one paw. She howled in agony, and we bounded like frightened deer from the spot, tearing our faces on the prickly branches in panic.

We stopped and listened. Only Trixie's whimpering disturbed the air. Craw considered. Who was the most fearsome, Henry or the trapper?

"The Gamie must be oot or his dugs would be barkin by noo," said Jackie.

We crept quietly back and with Jackie and I poised for flight, Craw puzzled as to how he could release the dog. He seemed to know about prisons, traps, chains and things. Soon he stood on the spring and Trixie was free. I don't think Henry every discovered how Trixie got a permanent limp. He questioned Jean. She blamed the garden fence. He suspected Craw but had no proof. Craw gained an enemy, Henry a more faithful friend for no "Rats or Fetchits," could entice Trixie with us again.

"Mr. Kilpatrick keeps the biggest dugs in the world," Jackie told us one day, "Hardly anyone's seen them as they're kept in his shed aw the time."

"Whit a shame," Craw replied, "They should be runnin aboot wi the rest o them in the streets."

Dogs were our companions of youth, usually mongrels, tail wagging, panting, laughing-eyed dogs, always ready to jump a fence, fetch a stick, chase a cat for us. Well bred dogs never seemed to last long in our street. One woman whose husband was a pay clerk in the pit offices, and therefore superior to miners, tried hard to keep an animal fitting to their social status.

She bought a golden spaniel first of all, with large limpid eyes and enormous paws. It lived about six months. The next was a dalmatian, a beautiful animal with markings like ink blots on white paper and a fine noble head. He did better. surviving nine months. She switched to cats after that. Seemingly the dogs had taken distemper, a word our parents used cautiously and fearfully much the same as the word rabies must be used abroad.

Only the occasional mongrel seemed to be affected and so rare as to draw a small crowd in the street as it lay kicking in spasms and foaming at the mouth. "Git back, git back,"an adult would shout, "It'll bite ye if ye touch it." Our street dogs came in all shapes and sizes, big ones, small ones, fat and thin ones. The real mongrel, or thoroughbred mongrel, if you like, was well proportioned, acquiring the best traits of various breeds, but some of their companions looked ludicrous where the dominant strains were too apparent.

One had a large alsatian head and short terrier legs, and another the sleek lines of the whippet adorned with coarse woolly fur. Many had no owners. A large black and white collie type arrived one day and slept on our back door step for a month. Mother gave him scraps and he raked the buckets to augment his diet. He jumped high fences as easily and gracefully as a show jumper and one day was gone as mysteriously as he arrived. Mongrel mating was a communal affair attended by most of the boys in the street. Someone would discover the two principal participants joined in wedlock and soon a small crowd would gather shouting encouragement or bawdy abuse. A small male and a large bitch came in for special applause. Most of the adults kept discreetly away, embarrassed, especially the owners. 'That's Tamson' s dug.' Henry's wife Jean acted as a sort of canine freedom fighter.

"Isn't that disgusting, Henry?"

She would march out with a pail of freezing water and fling it like a shower of confetti over the doggy duo and anyone else within range.

It has been observed that men choose dogs similar in looks to themselves and a few partnerships certainly bore out this theory. One villager had a pet, three quarter bulldog. He himself had a prominent lower jaw with a bottom tooth protruding upwards and sad, baggy eyes. The men with the whippets were lean, pale, big chested, narrow hipped and walked with their charge at an astounding pace.

I questioned father about Mr. Kilpatrick's big dogs. Yes, he had seen them occasionally being exercised at night or when we were at school. This only added to the mystery.

They're like elephants, father told me, but then he always exaggerated. A dug's a dug, I thought, and surely they couldn't be much bigger than Wilson's collie.

Jackie heard that one was called Horatio. What sort of name was that for a dog?

Most people called their dogs Rover, Roy or Rex and the bitches Trixie, Lassie or Flossie. Horatio indeed. Many cats didn't even get a name."That's oor cat," was quite sufficient a description.

On an appointed evening we waited until it was dark and. the moon came out. Craw climbed up the wall first, toes and fingers digging into cracks in the stonework,. then pulled Jackie and I up. Craw detailed me to stay on top of the wall as look out. I didn't argue. What if the dogs were as big as it was rumoured?

Craw and Jackie dropped down as lightly as cats. That was as far as they got. Out of the darkness padded a monster as big as a pony, the moon in its eyes and a tongue like a tawse. It came at them without a sound, more frightening than any barking and they froze to the wall. Craw and Jackie stood side by side, yet it managed to plant a massive paw on either side of them. They screamed in terror then, and a man came running round the side of the shed shouting "Down boy, down!"

The brute licked the boys faces in turn, like a cow at a salt block and released them from its hairy embrace. I was sternly ordered down into the garden. Mr. Kilpatrick saw that we were terrified and, after our initial fright had subsided, took us to see the other two dogs in the shed. They were Saint Bernards, he told us, very affectionate and often used to rescue lost travellers in the Alps. A saint was the last thing the first dog rushing at us looked like, more like the monster guarding the gates of Hell in a school poem I had read.

"Come back and see the doggies again," Mr. Kilpatrick offered graciously, "but next time, use the front entrance."

He gave us an apple each from one of his fruit trees, surely the safest trees in the whole of Kelty.

Benarty

THE WAR

I can vaguely remember the day the war started. I was six years old and not too concerned, but aware of my parent's anxiety and tension as they listened intently to the wireless. It was a Sunday, a quiet pleasant day, and Benarty gazed down on the village as strong and ageless as ever. It was inconceivable that life had changed in any way, and indeed for a while everything seemed fairly normal, the changes gradual.

At school we were fitted with gas masks and carried them everywhere, hanging from our necks in little brown boxes. At regular periods we practised putting them on. This was an unpleasant experience. I felt claustrophobic, trying to draw in air in big gulps with cheeks caving in and disliking the strong rubbery smell. The eyeshields misted up, my chin felt wet and my fellow pupils looked like aliens from another planet.

The sirens started practising and this was frightening and ominous, a sound of its own, the wail of the banshee, rising to a crescendo then fading away, leaving an uneasy stillness in the air. The birds were hushed for a while afterwards and the air seemed stunned and apprehensive. Father made blackouts for the window with strips of wood and thick card.

Fruit became very scarce and an apple was a prized treat. Hardly any boys ate an apple on their own.

"Gie's yir runt," a pal would shout and scrutinize the owner carefully until a reasonable core was reached. Sometimes it would be a triple ceremony, an enormous first bite to one pal, an uneasy interlude of eating by the owner for a short period, then the runt to another impatient participant.

Sugar and milk were replaced with sacharrins and dried milk. We obtained ration books and identity cards. Better off relatives gave my mother second hand clothes in exchange for clothing coupons and this saved her quite a bit of money. They say that a lot of people ate better during the war than they had ever done before. Once they knew they were entitled to certain portions of butter, meat, cheese and eggs, they felt obliged to take the full quota often in excess of what they had bought before. Mother lined the four of us up every morning and, like nestlings, we stood with open mouths for a teaspoon of horrible cod liver oil, followed by the antidote, a spoonful of concentrated orange juice.

An uncle staying with us at the time could consume half a bottle of cod liver oil in one gulp. He was a drinker and I suppose this was just another lubricant for his dry demanding throat.

A notice came round informing my parents of all the regulations and instructions pertaining to civilians. One suggestion was that the foundation of the house be converted into an air raid shelter until communal shelters could be built on selected sites. Father cut a hole in the floor of our bedroom cupboard and fitted a trapdoor. He also knocked down part of the wall in the outside coal cellar to allow another access to the foundations. Old rugs, coats and blankets were used to line an area between two dwarf walls. The shelter was about two feet six high, dark and musty, with unfamiliar smells and textures of brick, mortar and. earth. After a while, the rugs became too damp and uncomfortable, not much better than the ground.

Father sat in the centre, leaning against a wall and controlling the sole source of light, a torch, candles being considered too dangerous in the confined space. All sorts of creepie crawlies scurried away if the narrow beam of light fell on them. The centipedes were the worst. A clipshear or a slater was tolerable, but a centipede running over your face or legs made you shudder in distaste. We huddled as close as possible to Father and the torch for warmth, light, human contact, and fear of the crawly kingdom lurking on the fringes of darkness.

As soon as the warning siren went off at night, Mother hurried us out of bed and, still in pyjamas or nightdresses, descended into the nether regions of the house. Pud's house next door had a foundation too low for a shelter so Pud, his mother and Craw joined us, entering through the outside coal house. It was always rather eerie when they arrived, a furtive scuffling first of all, followed by the cold glare of their torch blinding us temporarily.

A black shape with three humps crawled along the dark tunnel towards us like a large loathsome grub with one eye only becoming familiar at the last moment. Parental anxiety transmitted to us and for most of the time we sat or lay subdued, talking in whispers as if the German pilots could detect louder voices. Craw sat stiffly apart from the group keeping his fears to himself. The all-clear siren had a different pitch, sounding friendly and cheerful. The effects of the two sounds were so different, the warning signal creating a feeling of panic with a tightness of the chest and throat while the all clear gave a sudden sensation of relief and relaxation. At first, the raids were

something of an adventure, then when we realised that they were going to be part of our lives for an indefinite time, an intrusion into our warm comfortable sleep at nights.

Soon the council erected communal shelters with two feet thick brick walls and flat concrete roofs. No families ever occupied the one nearest us during raids. The boys used it as a urinal during the day and it smelled infinitely worse than the foundation of the house. It achieved notoriety as a thieves den, a place for boys to carry stolen strawberries, turnips, and peas; swear, smoke and entice the bolder girls, foolish enough to enter. In fact, it was used for any purpose other than the one intended. Some mothers thought the shelter offered more dangers than the whole of the German Air Force.

A few incendiary bombs were dropped in the Forestry Commission woods, and quickly put out by the Civil Defence. Then came the night of our biggest fright. We were huddled as usual in the shelter when the drone of a plane was heard overhead, followed by the whistling of a bomb and a loud explosion. The house vibrated slightly and we crouched lower in fear. The whole village trooped out in the morning and in a field next to the Black Burn a great crater yawned. A cow and several sheep lay dead, their legs bent into unnatural positions. I gazed at the grotesque corpses, suitably impressed. Something that could kill an animal as large as a cow must be, indeed, dangerous.

Pieces of shrapnel lay scattered about and the children started scrambling for small pieces of the twisted metal as souvenirs. This was the closest we got to the war and the raids stopped shortly afterwards. The only casualty we heard of was four miles away in Kingseat, where a solitary bomb scored a direct hit on a house, killing an old man who lived alone.

Servicemen became our heroes. When they came home on leave the children pestered them for autographs, cigarette cards, uniform badges and buttons. A Polish Army camp sprang up at Cantsdam, on the outskirts of the village, and the Poles became an added attraction. Our autograph books started to fill with strange unfamiliar spellings and their buttons and badges were prized possessions.

They were heroes to the children, though not to the men of the village. The Poles had a way with women, especially the officers. The clicking heels and perfect manners were worlds apart from "Can ah see ye hame, hen?" or "Di yi fancy a pudden supper?"

Fights broke out at the local dance halls. Several of the soldiers married local girls, stayed on after the war and integrated well into the community, most being hard working, resourceful men, willing to attempt a variety of jobs.

We worked with Italian prisoners of war at the tattie howking, sad, sallow, dark-eyed men, wistfully showing us crumpled photographs of their families. They were kind and considerate, enjoying the company of children as substitutes for their own, pointing at the snapshots, then at us, indicating that we were roughly the same age. The prisoners were allowed an astonishing degree of freedom, sometimes unaccompanied by guards. The camp was situated near my Granny's house at Black Dub and a lorry picked them up in the morning and dropped them off at night. One of my cousins married a soldier who helped to guard the camp.

As most of our family worked in the pits we had very few close relatives in the forces. A cousin of my father's on embarkation leave visited us. He was over six feet tall, a sergeant-major in the Scots Guards, and the finest soldier I had ever seen. All eyes were drawn to the starched khaki uniform, chest ribbons and immaculate boots. He seemed to dominate our sitting-room effortlessly, emitting an aura of calm and authority I had never experienced before. I never saw him again. He was killed in France during the Normandy landings.

Our house was always overcrowded during the war. Although very little building was going on, babies were still being born, grandparents getting old and requiring attention. Granny Jones died and Granny Douglas moved in beside us. As our house had only two bedrooms, she occupied one, the four children another, and Father and Mother slept in a big bed in the living room.

The war brought out great camaraderie in the village and everyone just adjusted to changes in their house population. We even had a lodger for a short period and he slept behind a temporary partition in our room. George was lots of fun and loved children. He was always willing to play table tennis, ludo or draughts. We enjoyed his company for about a month then one day he was gone, taking Mother's rent money, which had been laid out on the sideboard, with him.

A hastily scribbled note informed Mother that he would return the money soon, and she had to borrow the rent from Granny who always had a bit extra. True to his word, after a fortnight had elapsed, George sent the money through the post, with a written apology. He was a decent chap really but a gambler and Father thought he was being pressed for a debt. Whether by intent or not, he always lost to us at draughts.

THE FAMILY

Mother was a great hostess and attracted lots of visitors. My earliest recollections of Braewell were of crowds, conversations and laughter with Father's voice booming out above the din. As a toddler, I remember at one stage, an enormous number of babies descending like a flood, sometimes literally, upon us. They didn't seem to have faces, only bottoms. As nurses remark, "Faces vary but all bottoms look alike."

The babies seemed to be permanently upended, while the mothers winded, wiped, polished and powdered. They drew the eyes unwillingly, in spite of a feeling of guilt, so undignified but fascinating in their absurdity. An indescribable odour filled the air, a mixture of nappies, milk, powder and Vaseline. With a final flourish, like a magician manipulating a large handkerchief, the mothers would tie a nappy, plug the baby's mouth with a dummy, and make it disappear into the labyrinths of a pram before I had time to study their upper features.

At meal times, I was dumped under the large, round mahogany table, out of the way, I suppose, of the fireplace and its bubbling pots and pans. It seemed to me like a large round cage with legs forming the spars. It was warm, dark and safe here with the light filtering through spaces between the sets of legs, constantly changing and flickering as the conversation ebbed and flowed. A hand would appear suddenly and thrust a treacle piece in my mouth. I loved treacle. In later years my favourite singer was Paul Robeson, a black American. My mother told me if I ate enough treacle, I'd look like him, so I ate piece after piece, checking my skin periodically to see if it was turning darker.

Once, a familiar face appeared above me. One of the visiting mothers had lifted her baby on to her knee, no nappy, no nothing, just the bare essentials. I couldn't resist the temptation, stretched upwards and sank my teeth into a chunk of flesh, a sort of hanging garden of babyland. An outraged howl stopped conversation dead. I was dragged out like a rabbit from a burrow and unceremoniously smacked. It was seventeen years before I saw the baby again. She visited Braewell as a smart attractive composed young woman. I hadn't the courage to ask her if the teeth marks were still there.

When Granny Douglas stayed with us many of her family would arrive on Saturday evenings and seats became very scarce, the children sitting on the floor wherever they could find a space. Exciting snatches of conversation drifted down, small leaves of gossip.

"She ran awa wi anither man leaving him and three bairns."

They always seemed to run. Did they never walk or cycle or catch a bus or a train with another man? Many of their women acquaintances seemed to be forever falling and strangely they knew exactly when they would be better.

"Aye, Mary fell at the New Year and she'll be better in September."

Would we ever understand the adult world? Hospitals and operations often dominated the conversation.

"They asked me to bring a sample of urine," an aunt exclaimed, "and the only suitable bottle I could find was an empty miniature whisky one. I shopped in Woolies before my appointment and would you believe it? Someone stole it from my shopping basket."

The room rocked with laughter. A big brawny cousin had a wife who was a keen spiritualist. After several persuasions he reluctantly accompanied her to a meeting.

"Never again," he cried, "The hall was in semi-darkness and the medium pointed straight at me. 'There's someone trying to contact you from the other side,' she told me. Did ah ken anyone with the initial J that had passed on? All of a sudden ah felt something touching ma leg under the bottom of ma troosers and fir the life o me ah kidnae look doon. The medium moved on and ah forced massel tae look. Wid ye believe it, a big black tam cat wis rubbin against me wi its tail stuck up the lig o ma breeks."

Father was unsurpassed as a raconteur, leaping to his feet and gesticulating appropriately to illustrate his accounts. He told the same stories time and time again, but was so entertaining that no-one minded. One of his favourites was the night in Lassodie when he took his dog, Peg, for a walk. They reached a ruined pit building, known locally as the haunted house, when suddenly 'Swoosh', something brushed father's head and the dog growled softly, flattening against the path.

He thought of all the tales of spooks and bogies he had heard since childhood and he turned to go back. 'Swoosh.' The unseen terror swept past again. He was about to run when the moon came out from behind a cloud and he saw the ghost. A big white barn owl was swooping on the dog. On another occasion at night the dog growled and braced its legs refusing to go any further along a track. This time the moon was out and nothing could be seen or heard. A small mound with a few stunted trees lay ahead. Peg was normally a very courageous dog and had killed young foxes, stoats, weasels and rats.

"Well, if you're feard, am feard tae," father whispered and returned the way they had come. He too had many hospital tales.

"Ah've had a bit o handlin in ma time," he remarked often.

Mother used to tease him about his ailments.

"You've got corns on your feet, then your bad ankle. Your knee gives way and you've had an operation for ulcers."

Moving up she described his bad chest and an arthritic shoulder. He had black luxuriant hair beyond reproach so she usually stopped at his headache caused by high blood pressure. One of his favourite medical tales was of a bachelor friend of his in Lassodie who stayed with an aged mother. Doctors had to be paid a fee when sent for, and most people had their own traditional cures passed on from parent to child. This man acquired a very painful boil on a buttock. His mother boiled the big black kettle on the fire then took a small bottle and filled it with steam from the spout.

"Noo, go intae the bedroom laddie and yase the wardrobe mirror tae see the boil. If ye pit the tap o the bottle against it, the hot steam will draw aw the matter oot."

He did as he was told, apprehensively. In a few minutes his mother leapt off her chair as a roar like a bull shattered the quiet.

"Ah canny stand the pain ony longer," he moaned, "That steam's far too hot."

He roared again in agony. His old mother burst through the door which had the back of a chair jammed against the handle and discovered her son, bent forward with the bottle stuck on the wardrobe mirror.

On many nights, twenty or so sat down to supper. Mother could make a meal faster than anyone I know. Her equivalent of the loaves and fishes were chips and beans, This, with lots of bread and butter, home-made jam and infinite pots of strong tea satisfied all. She had the wonderful ability to make a simple meal look like a feast, the tablecloth spotlessly white and a center piece of fresh garden flowers. Afterwards there was always at least one pianist, a mouth organist and a variety of singers to provide entertainment.

We children appreciated all the singers, some because they had fine voices and others because of their peculiarities. One uncle sang through his nose, to save his false teeth, they said, and always made several starts, muttering 'too high' or alternatively 'too low' and invariably blamed the pianist for playing too loud and drowning his, as he thought, deep manly voice.

There was always the self-styled shy person who had to be bullied and cajoled into singing and then was very difficult to stop. One uncle was always asked to sing 'Be kind tae auld Granny.' I don't think Granny was that old at the time and she was certainly quite   fit. The sad words of the song filled the room 'Be kind tae auld Granny, for oh she is frail, like a wind scattered tree bending low in the gale.' Poor Granny had to sit silent and solemn trying to look like a frail, wind scattered tree.

In the house the children had lots of freedom. The furniture was old and we were allowed a certain amount of horseplay and gymnastics such as forward rolls on the couch and headstands against the door. One object was sacred, the wireless. Father guarded this jealously as his main link with the wide world, and woe betide anyone who fiddled with the knobs. During the war, of course, parents listened intently to all the news bulletins and the children were told to keep absolutely quiet. The light coloured wireless stood on the bookcase, next to the fireplace and slightly above father's armchair so that he could act a protector and controller. Once, when he was out, a brash cousin carelessly put a cigarette end on the wireless and it left a small black mark. Father was furious when he returned and banished his nephew from the house for about three months.

'Never darken my wireless again.'

Our programmes were carefully selected. The McFlannels were a great favourite and as a special treat on Tuesday nights we were allowed to stay up late to hear 'Appointment with Fear,' introduced dramatically with the words, 'This is your story teller, the man in black' and eerie music in the background. We crawled fearfully to bed afterwards asking if the bedroom door could be left open for a while. A British Boxing championship was a great event and Father and I sat enthralled at the fireplace transported right to the ringside by grand commentators such as Raymond Glendinning and Barrington Dalby.

When we had visitors mother's raspberry jam was in great demand. Collecting the berries was one outing she made compulsory, and had favourite patches in the woods where the berries were large and plentiful. We would be given a two pound jar each and told "We'll go home after that's filled."

Some of the berries were difficult to reach, surrounded by nettles and other plants; brambles tore at your clothes and a plant we called 'sticky willie' deposited its tendrils on contact. Nettles were by far the worst, large weals appearing on the skin in no time. In time honoured fashion, we rubbed the sore parts with large docken leaves, grateful for the cooling effect and thinking the juices had magical properties.

Mother taught us the names of many of the wild flowers and trees and we recognised and ate strawberries, gooseberries, blaeberries, the sweet end of grasses and the leaves of a plant we called 'Soor Jimmies.' Unrecognised berries, mushrooms and other fungi were left untouched. Apart from docken leaves, the only other nature cure I remember trying was the milky substance found in the stems of dandelions, which I rubbed on several warts on my fingers. They turned black then gradually faded. I've never had warts since.

At last the jars were full, one each from the children while Mother had collected as much as the four of us in her basket. We showed her the damage, hands scratched and swollen.

"A cleg bit me," my youngest sister wailed.

"Oh, never mind," Mother smiled, "Wait till you taste the jam."

First the berries had to be cleaned. They had tiny white grubs we called mawks in them and these had to be picked out carefully without damaging the berries. This was a painstaking, boring task and many escaped the scrutiny. Father said that they added to the flavour, much superior to the jam made from cultivated raspberries. Mother's jam had a real tang, the taste of wild places, the haunt of the bee and the butterfly, of green languid pools and scented larch, or perhaps entirely due to the little white mawks.

After the sugar had been added and the jam boiled in a big aluminium pan, a glorious smell pervaded the kitchen making the jaws clap in expectantly and saliva moisten the mouth. We ate the first jarful before it had time to cool, on fresh white bread with a thick black crust and argued as to who would lick the big wooden spoon. These kitchen odours linger long in the memory; treacle scones, hot and dripping with butter, doughrings covered with sugar, apple fritters burning the hasty tongue.

Perhaps our greatest treat was a toffee apple. This is one of these rare combinations like peaches and cream, frying steak and onions, the twinning perfect. Mother's milky white apples, covered with light brown toffee, thick at the top where they had rested, were miniature masterpieces, melting in the mouth, the stick licked clean till not a trace remained. Perhaps the one childhood gourmet delight adults seldom try is the scorched potato. Some evenings when father burned his garden refuse, mother would give us a large potato each. These were placed in the fire, covered with sticks and left until black. When they were brought out they were literally too hot to handle, and flung from hand to hand in an effort to cool them quickly. The potatoes were always raw in the centre but the three outer coats of black, brown and half an inch of white, absolutely delicious.

Mother kept an open house, no one was turned away. During the war and afterwards, many drifters arrived and departed. Father said that they had a secret sign marked near our house saying 'Welcome' in Romany language. An old man with a khaki greatcoat, a tartan tammy and a ragged red beard would parade in front of the house, singing in the most broken and pathetic of voices, glancing wistfully at the window till mother asked him in for a bowl of soup and twopence.

We often arrived from school at lunchtime to find an old tinker woman with some of her family installed in the scullery. She praised us in the most ingratiating whine "My, whit bonny bairns, hoo auld is that wee lass? Ten? Same age as ma wee Hughie. Whit a braw family. Kin ye spare a wee drap dry tea? Thank ye, yir awfy kind. Hiv ye any auld clothes, ma wee Jean is aboot the same size as that wee'est ane o yours. Whit bonny een she has."

And so it went on. Her grey hair was dyed red, her skin like the hide of an aged horse but her teeth fascinated us more than anything, broken stumps, yellow, brown or black according to the state of decay. As the old lady couldn't write, mother asked me if I would fill in her ration books for her. I was flattered at the unexpected status and asked grandly "Name? Age? Address?" I was doing fine until reaching 'occupation' and glanced enquiringly at Mother who, slightly flustered said "Housewife." The old woman nodded happily in agreement. Anyone less like a housewife would be hard to imagine.

Our most regular character was a man known as Whistling Johnny, who was about thirty at this time and had a smooth boyish face and soft feminine hands. He walked with long jerky strides, whistling loudly and tunelessly. His visits were always perfectly timed, just before lunch. My sisters detested him, but I found him fascinating as he burst into convulsions of laughter at the feeblest of jokes, rocking in his chair, feet bouncing on and off the floor.

Johnny sold religious books and tracts, occasionally doing light work on farms. Mother told us he was delicate, which didn't seem to extend to his appetite. He would bring her a dozen collars at a time to be washed and ironed and was always immaculately dressed; black boots gleaming brightly. A visitor, recently widowed, asked him what size of boots he took as her husband had left a pair nearly new.

"Oh, anything about seven, eight, nine or ten," said Johnny enthusiastically, adding hopefully, "Thon wis a braw suit he wore on a Sunday."

He lived in a derelict cottage next to the Gairney Burn with his old senile mother and several half wild cats. All the washing was done in the burn and the cottage had no glass in the window frames but these and the doorway were covered with old rugs and sacks. To see Johnny dressed you would never imagine that he came from such a ruin.

Two men cycling home from a drinking session in Kinross stopped at the cottage one night attracted by the lead flashings on the chimneys. They climbed up a makeshift ladder and started prising off the lead with a screwdriver. Johnny and his mother woke up, frightened at the strange noises from the roof, and he went out to investigate, wearing one of his mother's long white nightgowns. When the men saw this fearful apparition, they half fell, half climbed off the roof and cycled off as fast as their legs could pedal.

When Johnny visited us, my mother always persuaded him to leave before father arrived home from work. Like my sisters, he didn't approve of the more colourful visitors. I was the only one who found them all fascinating, living in worlds I could only guess at.

The last we heard of Johnny, he had just escaped drowning in Southern Ireland. Some villagers threw him in a river when he tried to sell them the King James version of the Bible. Mother never turned anyone away without some food or money, even though she had so little to run the house on herself. In her youth she knew an old tramp called Jimmy Peely, who slept near the warm kilns of Blairadam Brickwork at night. He eventually landed in the Workhouse, which later became the Northern Hospital in Dunfermline, and Mother sometimes took me with her to see him, a gentle old man, still longing for the road and hating his white starched captivity.

Here she became acquainted with Bessie, a young woman who had been abandoned there as a child. Bessie was perfectly normal and had met a young gardener who wanted to marry her. Mother wrote several letters to the authorities and eventually they reluctantly agreed to release her providing Mother signed a form agreeing to be the girl's guardian.

The wedding took place and Mother lent Bessie her best coat for the occasion. That was the last she saw of the girl, her husband or her coat. Father was furious when he found out.

"If ye clap stray dugs, yir bound tae get bitten," he told her.

At holiday times, the house filled with more occupants. Cousins arrived in turn to stay for a week. Two older girls in their early teens arrived from Perth and joined us in our small bedroom. As they undressed for bed I was fascinated to discover that they wore and slept in white combinations, one piece suits with a long row of buttons down the centre.

I realized that I had a lot to learn about girls and kept unusually quiet, five to one was very oppressive. That night my bed had been moved next to the window to allow room for an extra mattress on the floor. A storm started and I lay terrified as the thunder clapped and lightning flashed across the sky, thinking that any moment I would be pierced with a long yellow sword. I never visualised myself being burned to a cinder or convulsing with electric shock waves, only being pinned to the bed like a butterfly in a collector's case.

My two young sisters lay fast asleep on the floor mattress. My eldest sister and two cousins called me over and I gratefully accepted though the awesome white combinations were nearly as terrifying as the lightning. The next day of course I was taunted for cowardice. Boys were supposed to be brave. Our sleep was to be disturbed yet again that week. On a fine evening Mother opened a window before putting the light out. We woke later, in pitch darkness, screaming, as furry bodies moved over the beds emitting unearthly wails. Mother rushed through and switched on the light. Four strange cats rushed to the window while our cat sat on a bed looking dejected at losing his friends.

Some nights we frightened each other with ghost stories. In Kelty the most fearful figure was the 'baffy man,' whose name conjured up a picture of an evil wolfish man wearing slippers to aid his speed in pursuit of victims.

"Be in before it's dark," some parents would say, "or the baffy man will catch you."

My sisters and I conjured up a trick to frighten the Perth cousins. I was last in bed and looped a length of string over the door handle leaving the door off the catch. As soon as I switched the lights off, my eldest sister told a tale of a haunted house building up the suspense until reaching my cue 'And suddenly the door swung open…'

There was a slight pause as I tugged frantically at the cord leading to my bed, then the door opened dramatically with a loud creak and everyone was duly frightened including my sister and I, as our imagination took over. In the evenings, if several visitors arrived, the children were sometimes asked to play in the lobby while the adults talked. This area was long and narrow and we played 'Blind Man's Buff.' All our coats hung on hooks here and they formed a great hiding place as, pressed hard to the wall, hardly able to breathe, we felt the fumbling hands of the 'blind men.' The girls were the noisiest, giggling or shrieking alternately, the boys quieter and more physical, jumping, pushing roughly, running too fast in the confined space. I was discovered behind a coat, hauled out roughly, and the large scarf tied round my eyes until I roared "It's far too tight."

"It's no,"

"You kin see noo," they said, as I frantically tried to slacken off the scarf which felt like a steel band. Eventually we reached a compromise and I was on my own, isolated in an exciting but frightening dark cocoon. Some cousins were bigger than me, and the lobby was fraught with dangers. Hands slapped me sharply on the face, the shoulder, the calves of the leg. I struck out blindly, grabbing cloth, only to find it being snatched out of my hand. Strange, soft unfamiliar shapes occasionally brushed my hands and I snatched them back quickly as giggles indicated the owners. The laughing, shrieking, banging and occasional crying would inevitably reach an intolerable crescendo and Father would suddenly appear, furious and usher us back into the living room again.

"Git back in there, the lot of yi. That racket wid waken the deid."

BLACK DUB

Before Granny Douglas came to stay with us, she lived in Black Dub cottage in a district known as The Fruix about four miles from Kelty. Her youngest son, Charlie, at this time in his late teens, stayed with her. I always spent part of the school holidays there away from the hustle and bustle of our crowded house. The cottage was low with a red pantiled roof and with an adjoining stable. There was no water supply, the water being drawn from a well or from a big barrel of rainwater outside the house, and the toilet was a little wooden hut next to the burn at the foot of the garden. There was no electricity, but the house was warm and cosy at night, the fire blazing away in the old black range, a big kettle always on the boil for hot water. The paraffin lamps gave a friendly glow to the room and had their own distinctive, though not unpleasant, odour. A black cat coiled cosily in front of the fire.

In the morning, the house was colder and I dressed quickly to keep warm. Granny told me to bring in a basin of water from the barrel and I washed myself at the sink. The water was freezing but exhilarating, and left the skin glowing. Visiting the hut at the foot of the garden was an ordeal. It was very primitive, just a wooden seat and and a pail. A nettle had curled itself under the door and lay poised ready to strike the unwary.

On a warm day flies buzzed noisily, and the strong odour was increased. Hens strutted about the midden close by and a few ducks quacked in the small burn. You certainly felt very close to nature here in more ways than one. It was not a place you were inclined to linger in long and, if daytime excursions weren't bad enough, darkness brought other terrors.

In the cottage across from Black Dub lived an old woman, bent and wizened, whom everyone said was mad. She hardly spoke to her neighbours and then only to curse them obscenely or accuse them of malicious acts towards her. I saw her occasionally working in her garden or peering suspiciously from a dusty window. She was always in my thoughts when I picked my way by torchlight to the hut. Each time I had to make an important decision, bolt the door for safety and be trapped inside or leave it open to escape. Like my plans, the little hut left very little room for manoeuvre.

"Are yi back already lad? My, that wis quick," Granny would say in amazement.

My uncle had inherited two things from his father, a liking for drink and an inability to take a bad bend with his bike afterwards. He drank late one night in a hotel in Kinross. The cook said "Here, take this home for breakfast tomorrow," and wrapped up some raw steak and mushrooms. Uncle placed them inside his shirt and buttoned it up then put his jacket on. He cycled home happily and had nearly reached Black Dub when he failed to take the bend, struck a tree and temporarily knocked himself out.

An old man and his wife, out for a walk, shone their torch and saw the bent bike and crumpled figure. They were horrified to see the bloody pulp of a chest as the steak and the mushrooms spilled out, and went for help as fast as their old legs could toddle.

When they returned, the body had vanished and in its place a large wolfish black dog stood licking its chops.

I loved Granny's breakfasts at Black Dub. She gave me thick porridge covered with cream, then a free range egg much bigger than the ones in the shop and with a lovely yellow yolk. My uncle took me for jackdaws' eggs to Cleish Crags , where the birds nested in every available fissure and hole. We collected about twenty or thirty eggs between us and returned home. One the way back to Black Dub we passed a mansion house and Charlie pointed out a big dog standing perfectly still on the lawn.

"Whistle and it will come over," said Charlie.

I whistled and shouted but the dog never moved. I then noticed Charlie nearly bursting with suppressed laughter.

"It's stuffed," he gasped eventually.

Seemingly the owners had been so fond of their pet that when the dog died of old age they took him to a taxidermist, so there he stood on the lawn, the perfect pet, requiring no food or drink, no walkies, just an occasional dusting with powder to discourage the bluebottles.

Charlie was great fun, always ready for a laugh or a prank. Once when he visited us at Kelty he swung my youngest sister to the ceiling and put her head right through the large glass light bowl. Father banned him for a while. Back at Black Dub we discovered a note from Granny saying that she had gone to visit her sister in Kinross.

Charlie said "We'll have a big omelette each but we'll hiv tae breck the jeckies eggs intae a cup first in case ony are turned."

We did this for a while but only a few showed slight spots of blood so the rest were broken straight into the frying pan, red spots and all. Charlie fried an enormous omelette and cut it carefully in half. It was delicious or at least in my hunger, it seemed that way. My friends and I often ate wilds birds' eggs, usually pigeons, waterhens and peewits.

Mother would patiently fry them for me but neither she nor the rest of the family would sample an egg. The week at Black Dub would always pass quickly but in a way

I was glad to return home to a house with modern facilities. I often felt that I had been away on safari.

Jackie, Craw and I saved up for weeks for a jaunt to Perth, twenty miles away. The bus journey seemed endless, Kinross, Milnathort, Glenfarg, Bridge of Earn then Perth. There were nearly always shows on the South Inch during the war and we made them our first stop. I was fascinated with the Roll the Penny stall, trying the coin at the top of the wooden chute, then the middle and so on. The man in charge always seemed to let you win at first even if the coin was slightly touching the line then inevitably you lost all your money.

Jackie and Craw arrived from the Big Dipper and Craw showed us how to tackle Roll the Penny. He went to a nearby tree and broke off a twig about two foot long. As soon as the man turned his back Craw moved our coins into the centre of the square. We won steadily for a while till the man, getting suspicious, turned quickly, saw the stick and chased us from the fairground. We tried the boats in the pond on the Inch then wandered to the centre of the city. We came across a treasure trove.

At that time, the Meal Vennel had several second hand shops and they were crammed with all sorts of exciting objects, fishing rods, knives, daggers, tools, clothes. An enormous bamboo spear caught my eye, about twelve feet long with a steel heart shaped head, a foot in length, decorated with tassels and markings. It was priced at five shillings, exactly the money that I had left. A few minutes later we left the shop, Craw the leader at the spear head, Jackie in the centre and I looked after the tail end. At Tay Street we came across our first obstacle, the Kelty bus conductress.

Many Kelty people were employed at Alexander's bus depot in Kelty and the garage was a prominent feature. Many of the long serving drivers were famous for their exploits. One damaged a double-decker bus trying to take it under a low bridge on the way to Bridge of Earn Hospital. Another hit and killed a cow near Crossgates. Ever afterwards, he was known as Rawhide.

The conductresses, or bus lassies as they were called, ruled their buses with rods of iron and hearts of gold. They sorted out everyone - unruly children, the drunks, moaners and groaners - in a firm but humorous manner. One girl jumped off her bus at the turning point at the top of the Black Road, forgetting it was going on to Kinross and not back to Cowdenbeath. The driver, unaware of her departure, drove off without her. She hitched a lift from the first person that came along, a man on a motorbike, shouting out, "Catch that bus."

 The bus lassies were very popular at local dances, the boys hoping maybe that they'd get a free hurl the next time they met on the bus. The lassies' hardest job was putting off reluctant passengers after the bus was filled to capacity, giving the contradictory cry. "C'mon. Get aff . "

"Yir no comin on the bus wi that thing," the conductress said, but she relented after a while and we manoeuvred the spear on to the single decker bus, passengers grabbing their hats or ducking down, mostly amazed by the proceedings. The spear at last lay along the passageway. We sat for an hour in the bus dreading reaching our destination and having to go through the same ordeal again. At last we stood outside the bus while the driver and the conductress fumed at the delay. The passengers grinned and waved at us for brightening up their long journey. We strode up the road in the same order as before, three Zulu warriors on the warpath in darkest Kelty.

Mother loved antique shops and jumble sales. She would have been in her element in the Meal Vennel amongst all the junk. She once bought an enormous oak mantelpiece and insisted, against the wishes of the family, on having in installed in our small living room. It certainly looked majestic when fitted in position, but rather overpowering in a small room. At a jumble sale with her I bought a beautiful bowler hat, all black and shining. The following day a widow, who had just recently lost her husband, visited my mother.

Catching sight of me wearing the hat and attempting a tap dance on the polished floor she said, "Kin ah see that a minute son? Wid ye believe it, that's Wullie's hat. I handed in aw his clothes tae the sale."

Bowler hats were scarce in Kelty. I didn't know what to say not knowing whether she was pleased that I had admired and bought it, or sad with memories of her departed husband.

Mother was only five foot tall and weighed about seven and a half stones, yet she worked like a Trojan, up at six every morning, last to bed at night, cooking, cleaning and washing for, at that time, eight people. She also tried to visit the old and the sick and helped them in any way possible. Only her indomitable will kept her going. She never complained or listened to advice. Father grumbled constantly about all the extra work she was doing and this only added to the pressure. One night she looked peculiar, an unfamiliar brightness in her eyes. She spoke fairly normally but, unlike her usual manner, very blunt and aggressive, listing all our faults.

The doctor arrived, put her under sedation and the ambulance stopped at our door the following morning. Mother was excessively cheerful. She turned to us and waved, saying "Well, I won't be back here again," and the ambulance moved on. We were desolate, a mother there one day, seemingly normal, the next a stranger with suspicious eyes and tight mouth. Luckily, she recovered quickly.

The doctor told us that she had allowed herself to get so rundown physically that the mind had finally made its protest. Father took us to the hospital to visit her a fortnight later and she was back to normal after undergoing electric therapy and bed rest. I'll never forget the visiting room. All the women wore coarse grey linen dresses, looking more like prisoners than patients. Some were absolutely senile while others were mentally defective. It must have been a nightmare for mother, becoming aware gradually of these grim surroundings.

As we spoke to her cackling laughter and animal noises broke out in corners of the room. I do not know how the authorities at that time expected anyone to recover in such circumstances. The patients could surely have been at least separated into long and short term. The whole atmosphere of the place was depressing and forbidding. Mother put on a brave front but desperately wanted to go home. Father went to the doctor who insisted that she stay another two weeks for complete rest.

My eldest sister coped very well. Father kept her off school and she did the housework, cooking and washing. Relatives and friends gathered round to help. Neighbours were understanding and sympathetic. Under the strain of wartime conditions, with rationing and overcrowding, many women had taken ill in a similar way to Mother. There was still a stigma attached however to mental illness and other children could be very cruel.

"Is it true yir mither's in the mad house?" one bold boy asked me in the street.

I didn't tell him I considered his mother permanently mad though she had never been for treatment to my knowledge. I was eleven years old and my world suddenly fearful and insecure. The loving Mother who was always there was there no longer. I felt so sorry for myself at school one day that I sat on the school steps and cried bitterly. Life was hard. Was Mother ever coming back? Was the war never going to end?

She arrived back one day, smiling and lively as ever. The house had been cleaned from top to bottom for her coming. Father had given us all chores to do. Granny had moved in with a daughter and mother got back to her own bedroom. She slowed down a bit after that, getting more sleep and not tackling so much work. We all tried to help a bit more and life returned to normal.

Benarty still gazed on us benignly, wise and remote from all human frailties.

Bus lassie – We've killed one o yer coos
Farmer – Bullocks
Bus lassie – No, it wis a coo

"... and who's gonnae mak me git aff, ah said."

PETS

We always had pets. Father had kept a large variety as a boy and encouraged us to do the same. Mother wasn't too keen on the animal kingdom but as always very tolerant. A real individual herself, she was not prone to stifle individuality in others. Inevitably, like all children, we were very enthusiastic when the pets were first acquired, then tended to neglect them as the novelty wore off and they represented a certain amount of work. I remember having a white rabbit that rose higher and higher in its hutch as the floor piled up with debris. When its ears touched the roof Mother said firmly "It'll have to go, you're not looking after it properly. The hutch hasn't been cleaned out in weeks."

I was secretly relieved and wanted to give it to a friend. Mother, always hard up, insisted that I try to sell it. No one seemed interested.

"Take it to the butcher and see if they'll buy it," Mother said.

Despite my pleas she was firm. "It's got to go."

So I trudged round the three butchers, Bayne's, The Argentine and the Co-operative. The interviews were very similar.

"Di yi buy rabbits mister?"

"Aye son, let me see them. Hi, that's a pet. Scram."

It seemed no butcher wanted a large white buck rabbit with red eyes. Eventually a local lad gave me a shilling for it. He wanted it to mate with his two does. So my rabbit landed lucky after all, bought for stud instead of stew. When Granny Douglas came to stay with us she brought a big collie called Major with her. We children adored him. He had a very shaggy black and white coat and was very strong. Granny had never managed to train him properly and he was one of those dogs who took children for a walk rather than the other way round, panting, foaming at the mouth, pulling at the lead, nearly choking himself. Father took him in hand. At first Major growled and snarled but Father stood no nonsense and the dog became fairly obedient walking quietly with the lead. We all went on a walk through the fields to Lassodie and Major became very excited at the rabbit scents.

There were no sheep in the field so Father let him off the lead. A rabbit bolted in front of us and the dog was off, yelping madly, disappearing over a hillock. Father hobbled after him as fast as he could manage. His fears were well founded. There was Major in the next field holding a sheep by the throat while the rest of the flock pranced madly away. The dog came obediently when Father called and he slipped him back on the lead giving the dog a hard smack on the head. A red faced farmer seemed to appear from nowhere and roared "Stand back, stand back, "I'm going to shoot that dug."

Major wisely hid behind my father. The girls were terrified and ran to Mother.

"You're shooting nae dug," Father said, "and get that gun pointed away fi me."

The farmer cooled down, then said "Oh, it's you John."

It turned out that they had been school friends. Father explained what had happened and the farmer strode off, slightly mollified but threatening further action if any of his ewes bore dead lambs. Major loved lying on the fireside rug, gazing into the flickering flames. His sight became poor, fire blind, someone told us. He started accidentally knocking down children in the street and after several complaints, father decided to give him away as a watch dog. His new owner lived at the other end of the village and Major returned the next day, a frayed rope dangling from his collar. The owner thought that he lived too near us and the dog would always try to escape, so another owner was found in Inverkeithing. Major panted in two days later and lay down at the fire while the children made a great fuss of him. He had travelled ten miles to come home.

We pleaded to keep him but Father said "No, he's getting too big and strong, and am fed up wi the neebors complainin."

An uncle in Perth knew a woman who owned a small shop at the edge of the South Inch and wanted a watchdog, so Major acquired yet another owner. His new mistress was very kind and fed him well. He received two rabbits a week from the butcher, plus other delicacies. Major was a very intelligent animal. He never attempted the twenty mile journey to Kelty.

When visiting Perth, my sisters and I used to always look out for him as the bus approached the South Inch. Occasionally we caught a glimpse of him waddling near the shop, very fat, but the picture of contentment. We pleaded for another dog and Father eventually acquired a black, shaggy mongrel. It was named Lucky. Why, I don't know. If suppose that if he could survive living with us he was lucky indeed. He was a lovable, affectionate animal with peculiar red eyes that glowed in the dark. Lucky was also religious, going to the Gospel Hall with my mother every Sunday and lying quiet at her feet during the service. He could even sing. When someone played the mouth organ, Lucky joined in with his own musical version, varying his whine with the change of notes, whether in irritation or pleasure no one was sure.

He loved to rake the buckets and gave the show away by coming home with a long grey beard and a guilty expression in his red eyes. His worst fault however was to roll in the garden manure and he would enter the house only to be driven off with shouts, kicks and thrown objects.

Later he would be put in the bath and scrubbed down with a stiff brush. Lucky was so shaggy that his silhouette could be seen on the light wallpaper just inside the living room door, as each part of him registered in turn as he brushed past. Father left for work early, about six in the morning, and would speak to the dog before leaving.

"Aye, it's awricht fir you lyin there snug in front o the fire while ah go oot intae the cauld."

He always swore that Lucky never moved a muscle except for a sly wink from one of the glowing red eyes. Father would take the dog for a walk most evenings and pass a group of buildings known locally as 'Coo Kates.' The owner had a small general store selling milk, vegetables, eggs, fruit and groceries. Next to the store was a byre, where she kept about twenty cows, which she looked after and milked herself. She was a very hard-working person which perhaps tended to make her a bit bad tempered.

A large black collie always lay outside the byre in the evenings, and he viciously attacked any dog that passed. He would approach very quietly, stiff legged, hair bristling and without any preliminaries, wade straight into a frenzied assault. Poor Lucky, no fighter, was badly bitten twice and Father complained to Coo Kate.

"That's twice that brute's guzzled ma dug."

Kate was very snippy, and during the war people depended on the goodwill of shopkeepers.

"Ye dinny hiv tae walk this way wi yir dug," she snapped and slammed the door. The next day Father cut a thick hawthorn stick and took his usual walk in the evening, this time with Lucky on the lead. Coo Kate's dog rushed out as usual and grabbed Lucky by the throat. Father laid her dog out with a perfectly placed blow to the head. I don't know whether it still attacked other dogs but when Father and Lucky passed by, it growled and grumbled but made no attempt to come to close quarters.

Lucky was joined for a few years by Dan, a cat Father got from a foreign ship in Rosyth Dockyard. The cat had an unusual blue grey fur and grew into a great hunter. No bird or mouse was safe in the garden as long as Dan was around. We watched him once from the window with a mouse that he had caught. He carried it to the middle of the lawn, placed it carefully on the short grass, walked slowly back a few paces, lay down and pretended to be asleep. The wet bedraggled mouse would recover slightly, see its chance and run for the vegetable patch. Dan timed it exactly. He would allow it to run for a bit but as soon as it was a yard from the patch he would streak from his spot and catch the mouse before it had time to escape. He repeated the performance a few times then, tiring of the game, tossed the rodent into the air and bit it fiercely as it fell down.

Like Major the dog, Dan jeopardised his own future. Being a tom cat he was always wandering at nights and, coming in to the house one morning soaking wet, soon had a bad cold. Father had a phobia about pets passing on colds to the children.

"Don't sniff in this family," Mother used to say, "or you'll be put down."

Father hadn't the heart to kill the cat so invited it for a walk one Sunday and left it in the middle of the Forestry Commission woods. Dan was gone for a year then turned up one evening on the window sill, sleek and fat, purring like a lion. We children were delighted, making a great fuss of him thinking what a clever cat he was, living wild in the woods all that time, hunting its own prey, avoiding foxes and traps. It was ten years before I discovered the true story. Dan had arrived hungry on the gamekeeper's doorstep and he had taken it in for a while. A visiting friend from the village had admired the cat and offered to give it a home.

"Aye it's a braw cat," the gamekeeper said "but ah'll dress it fir ye first tae stoap it fae strayin."

Dan was duly castrated and given to the new owner, who lived at the other end of the street from us. As soon as the cat found himself in familiar surroundings he returned home, none the worse, or should I say, only slightly the worse for his wanderings. The family never noticed any difference in him except that he seemed to prefer staying in at nights. We put it down to old age. Dan was luckier than our neighbour Spike's cat, who was hit by a van and badly injured. The cat was crawling about the garden, mewing pitifully and Spike asked my Father to shoot it. Father took out his double-barrelled shotgun and put the poor animal out of his misery. Some of the other neighbours heard of the incident and asked Father if he would dispose of their unwanted cats.

"Naw, naw," he told them, "Ah'm shootin nae cat wi nothin wrang wi it."

Spike lived near us. He was big, a strong man among strong men. He worked in the pits but had done time in the army and reached the finals of the regiment boxing championships. Like really strong men he was gentle, with nothing to prove. The only time he could be induced to show his strength was after a drink. A large boulder stood outside the Ex-Servicemen's Club, and Spike was the only man who could lift it clear off the ground. A truss club had been formed for those who tried but failed.

At the Gala Day Spike was automatic choice as anchor in the colliery team and if he was on the rope, the bandsmen or the Co-operative team had no chance. He took me fishing with him sometimes to the Gairney as his ghillie. Those massive hands could lift rocks but were not designed to put a wriggling maggot on a fly hook. He never caught anything, at least when I was there. I don't think Spike minded, the trout had never done him any harm. We sat on the banks of the Gairney, a gentle giant and a small boy, listening to the sound of the water, and the sighing of the cushy doos, with Spike joining in occasionally in that deep marvellous voice – 'Old Man River, You just keep rolling along,' Spike had a deep baritone voice in great demand at concerts. Even the doos hushed in admiration at this strange songster in their midst.

Spike had three sons of his own but they were chased off to the army as soon as they came of age. He didn't want them down the pits, and who knows, he had taught them well enough and one might win the heavyweight boxing division. When my father had his horrendous accident down the pit, it was Spike who reached him first, who moved the great stone with his bare hands and dragged him to safety, ignoring the small stones and dust still falling ominously on to his bare shoulders. Yes, we owed a lot to Spike.

"Here, tak this turnip and cabbage ower tae Spike," my father would say, or "Away and gie him a hand tae clean oot his doos."

The crib lay at the bottom of his garden, painted green and white. His birds, unlike Pud's scrawny pet, were lovely. They strutted about on the flight deck cooing softly, puffing up their chests, the sun picking out surprising blues and greens in their glossy feathers. Spike held them as gently as a mother with a baby. Cradled in the strong, blue scarred hands, the doos lay still, safe, protected - back in the egg.

JAKE

Once, when I visited Black Dub, my uncle had a pet jackdaw. It was an engaging bird, coming to his call and following him all over the garden. He had it six months, then it flew into the Italian prisoner of war camp in the field next to them and was never seen again. Perhaps they ate it to supplement their diet. I was enchanted by the jackdaw and determined to get one myself.

Jackie and Craw offered to accompany me to the Cleish Crags where the birds nested in their hundreds. We pumped up the bike tyres outside Braewell Cottage and changed into sandshoes for climbing.

"Kin a come wi ye?" a voice asked.

It was Alex Napier or, as we called him, Neep. He was almost bound to be called Neep. Apart from his surname, his head had the look of a turnip, flattening out at the top with a crop of hair sprouting upwards from the centre. He was tall with the long gangling gait of the born runner. He had all the qualifications, able to run like the wind, climb like a monkey, and in fact there was something ape-like about him. His hands looked nearer his knees than his hips. He would make a good adventurer.

We cycled down the Black Road, along the Great North Road for several miles, under the shadow of Benarty, then turned left at Blairadam Station. Soon the Cleish Crags came into view, a grey slash in the countryside, with broken, dangerous rocks. At the foot lay many boulders, some as big as table tops, wedged against a dry stane dyke. They had all slipped out of the cliff face and rolled down.

A steep, grassy slope with sheep tracks, and riddled with rabbit burrows, led to the crags which in places were nearly vertical. The jackdaws nested in practically every crack and crevice large enough for occupation. Some of the crevices were deep and over the years the birds had added to the twigs, sheep wool and paper so that some nests were at least six feet high. The jackdaws, very gregarious birds, even nested in the rabbit burrows to stay in the colony. Hundreds of them flew into the air as we climbed the grassy slope, loudly clacking and swinging upwards in the air current. Some gave us a fright as they exploded from the entrance of rabbit burrows we grasped to pull ourselves up.

We paused at the top of the slope and sat down. The aspect was magnificent. Below us lay fields and farms with horses, cows and sheep like polka dots in a multi-coloured dress. The Gairney coiled lazily beyond. To the right Benarty rose majestically over the sparkling water of Loch Leven and honking gaggles of geese rose and fell like clouds of dust in the neighbouring fields.

Craw, the first to get his breath back, took out his chanter and played 'The Rowan Tree,' very appropriately, as several rowans clothed the hillside, some even sprouting out half way up the steep face of the crags. Lady Nairn's sad old Scottish song echoed in the hollow of the rocks 'There isna sic a bonny tree in aw the countryside.'

The jackdaws puzzled as to what sort of invaders were trespassing their domain, and the lambs on the grassy slope ran bleating to their mothers. We decided to split up.

Craw and Neep wanted to explore a ledge further along the crags from where a kestrel had flown. A hawk's nest was rare and seldom accessible. The jackdaws mobbed the bird as soon as it rose and it flew down to the shelter of the woods.

Jackie and I climbed high, side by side, the broken rock and small trees jutting out providing toe and finger holds. A jackdaw flew out of a crevice to the right of us so we edged along in that direction, Jackie leading. He found a narrow ledge and this helped his progress for a while until he came to a gap of about a yard in length. Jackie paused, then jumped across, slipping on the other side and disappearing from sight over the outcrop of rock.

He yelled once then all was quiet. I felt sick with apprehension and grasping a branch above me, leaned outwards and peered down, fearing the worst. Jackie was sitting up in a large patch of nettles, rubbing his stings.

"Ah'm aw richt," he gasped, the breath knocked out of him.

I moved cautiously to the gap and, noticing a small bush at the other side, jumped and took hold of a branch at the same time. I was safely over. Jackie stood below, blinking his eyes at the gap, expecting me to come crashing down beside him. The ledge sloped upwards. I didn't want to go any higher, neither did I fancy jumping the gap again. It looked wider from my new position. There was nothing else for it but to move upwards and hope to find an easier way down.

Another bird flew out in a flurry of feathers, this time from a crevice just ahead of me. I peered in and saw a young jackdaw, all on his own, feathered and just the right

age for taking. He cawed raucously as I slid my hand in, thinking it was a parent returning and opened a wide, yellow beak in expectation, violently quivering his wings. I grabbed him before he could retreat further into the crevice, and buttoned him up inside my shirt to leave my hands free for climbing.

"Ah'v goat wan," I shouted delightedly to Jackie, busy with a large docken leaf below.

A tree hugged the cliff face not far from where I stood and I moved towards it thinking I could perhaps climb down its branches for the rest of the way. A large rock blocked my way and grasping hold of it, I edged round slowly on the ledge moving one foot at a time, facing the rock but leaning slightly outwards to avoid crushing the young bird which was starting to protest inside my shirt. The rock, bigger than I was, moved slightly. I couldn't believe it, I thought it must be only the jackdaw pushing against my chest. I clung to the rock feeling slightly giddy. The next moment it slid slowly out of its seating and forced me backwards into space.

I landed awkwardly on a broad ledge several feet down, and the rock bounced over my head, went to the base of the crags and rolled down the grassy slope to join other boulders at the bottom.

Again the jackdaws rose in alarm and filled the air with their clamour. Sheep near the path of the boulder   dashed wildly about. Standing up, my legs shook uncontrollably and I sat down again, closed my eyes, and offered a short prayer for my deliverance. Jackie's anxious voice pierced the air.

"Ir ye awricht up there?"

I tried my legs again. "Aye, Ah'm fine," I answered in an unsteady voice.

Miraculously the young jackdaw seemed unhurt but a soggy mess inside my shirt indicated his protest at flying through the air without previous tuition from his parents. One good thing, I was much nearer to the base of the Crags now and I climbed down carefully to join Jackie below. Craw and Neep appeared.

"What's goin on here?" Craw asked, ""Ah thocht you twoh wir startin an avalanche."

"Aye, and we were nearly knocked doon bi a stampede o sheep," Neep added.

He held up a kestrel's egg delightedly. "There wis twoh so we kept wan, and Craw said ah could have it."

They all admired the young jackdaw, which showed no fear, but sat still on my arm.

"It's ta'en a fancy tae yi, Jimmy." Craw said, "It even thinks yir shirt's its nest bi the look o it."

"Play the retreat on yir chanter," Jackie cried, "It's time we goat oot o here."

Craw obliged and piped us down the hill, the enormous boulders at the foot taking on a new significance. We came to a small square reservoir, perhaps related to a nearby farm water supply. We were all filthy and sweating, covered with dust, strands of sheep wool and burrs from plants.

"Last wan in's a lassie," Neep roared and we flung off our clothes in unison and dived into the freezing water, catching our breath with the sudden shock, then glorying in the exhilaration and freedom of swimming unfettered. An angry roar shattered the idyll.

A farmer came running down the grassy slopes of the crags with two collies yelping at his feet. We clambered hastily out of the water and ran down the field naked, clutching our clothes, the jackdaw still wrapped up in my shirt. As soon as we had gained a reasonable distance from the farmer we put on our pants, falling over each other in tangled disarray then ran again as the yelping dogs approached. Another quick stop to don a vest and we were off again. We reached the road where we had hidden our bikes behind a hedge and cycled for half a mile before fully dressing.

"We showed that auld deucher hoo tae run," Craw grinned.

"Aye, bit his dugs must hae been gae auld tae or they wid hae got us," Neep observed.

At least the road was public property. We cycled home slowly in quiet companionship, two abreast, the road smooth and soothing after the rough terrain of the Cleish Crags. Craw and Jackie started howling with laughter behind Neep and me.

"Whit's sae funny?" Neep asked, turning his head.

"Yiv goat yir troosers oan back tae front," they told him simultaneously.

Jake was the best pet I ever had. When I arrived home from Cleish, Mother gave me a cardboard box and said that he could stay in the house for one night only. I placed some old newspapers in the bottom to give him a soft bed and to catch his droppings. Father inspected the bird with a professional air.

"Gie um some breed soaked in milk," he told me, " That'll dae um fir a week or twoh."

Jake was hungry, but puzzled, when a white beak appeared above him, actually two of my fingers, not the same shape and colour as his mother's and dripping a white liquid. He refused to open his beak at first so I prised it open and placed a piece of bread well back in his throat. He made no attempt to swallow so I squeezed his beak shut cutting off the air supply and he swallowed violently, the scrawny neck undulating with the effort.

The bread and milk was to his liking. He wanted more. This time there was no hesitation and he sucked strongly at my fingers extracting the last drop of milk. I fed him until he was satisfied, milk drooling from the sides of his beak and his eyelids dropping over the vivid blue eyes as he fought with sleep.

I got up early the next morning. Too many pets brought in from the wild are dead the next day, to the great disappointment of their owners.

"They will themselves to die," Father used to say, surveying the stiff body of a young greenfinch or bank vole. I approached the cardboard box in the scullery fearfully and looked in.

'Yak, Yak.' There was no mistaking the urgent call for food. Jake stretched his scrawny neck upwards, yellow beak wide open and wings quivering in expectation. This time he could hardly wait to get the bread down, gulping greedily and opening his beak again before the piece had disappeared down the yellow chasm. In the afternoon I took him outside and placed him in the grass where he crouched, fearful of his new open surroundings. I crouched low too and spoke to him, holding out my arm.

"Jake, Jake, c'mon Jake."

Already he knew my voice and came hopping to the only familiar thing in the strange world he found himself in. I offered a wrist, pressing it to his breast bone. He protested at this liberty but clambered up clumsily on to my wrist, his claws making long white scratches in my skin. Jake now seemed to accept me entirely as his sole parent.

Father gave me the use of a small shed at the bottom of the garden next to a high stone wall after taking out a few gardening tools and putting them in to the coal cellar. Jackdaws called in the trees next to the Black Burn so perhaps Jake wouldn't feel too lonely and I kept him in his cardboard box for a while. At first he looked very comical.

He was already well feathered but had a fat bare tummy, the skin seeming to be tightly stretched like a drum over his internal organs.

The grey head of the mature jackdaw was already starting to emerge; his beak was long and sharp with the young bird's s tell-tale large yellow hinge at the base and feathers like stiff hairs on top of the beak near the head. His legs and feet were very black with long hooked claws. His most prominent features, however, were his eyes, the most wicked, mischievous, startling blue eyes I had ever seen on a bird, or a human for that matter. Occasionally, light grey top eyelids closed like blinds, while he sat solemnly looking as if he was pondering on some serious matter. Like all jackdaws, he had a slightly musty vinegary odour, different from other birds.

Soon Jake half flew, half scrambled to the top of his box and it was time to give him some more space. I fixed a series of spars across the shed, one six inches off the floor, finishing with one about five feet or so. Jake progressed in a fortnight to the top spar and soon roosted there every night. He would hear my footsteps on the garden path long before I reached the shed in the morning and begin a great clamour. As soon as I opened the door he flew straight on to my arm, very agitated, cawing, flapping his wings, demanding food then gulping greedily as if he was starving.

After feeding him, I left the remainder of the scraps in a dish and soon he picked clumsily away, dropping most of the food at first then gradually gaining expertise. He always wanted to be fed by hand for part of the meal and this habit remained with him all of his life, gaining some sort of comfort from the contact of beak and fingers. His wings grew stronger quickly and soon he was a proficient flyer.

Jake changed his routine now. As soon as I opened the shed door in the morning he flew straight out and soared to the top of Braewell Cottage. I walked down the path a few paces, held out an arm and called "Jake, Jake."

He nearly always came straight away, gliding down, stalling at the last moment then grasping frantically at my arm for a grip. After several attempts he mastered the landing and executed the whole of the flight in a smooth effortless action. This is one

of the great thrills in keeping a jackdaw, calling a wild creature from the skies and watching it grow bigger and bigger as it approaches its owner, no hesitation, complete trust in a human being.

Although Jake would occasionally hop on to other arms looking for titbits, he would only answer my call, a one boy bird. He only allowed me to touch his head, a part he couldn't reach easily himself and would sit perfectly still as I scratched it, his eyes closed in ecstasy and tiny skin flakes like dandruff floating downwards. He allowed me to could stroke him gently on the back and wings, but hated to be lifted bodily, protesting loudly, the nape feathers of his head rising in anger. This part of his wild heritage he never surrendered.

SCHOOL

I hated the school, the teachers, with one or two exceptions seemed old and crabbit, some recalled from retirement when the War started, the lessons dull and uninspiring. I received the belt hard and often usually for dreaming, in my mind's eye seeing the cool waters of the Gairney at Cleish and the trout rising to the dancing midges. Some of the spinster teachers were the worst, boys a continual reminder of the sex that had ignored or rejected them. Married women with children of their own were noticeably more mellow.

Fritz was the terror of the school. He was German and spoke in a thick guttural accent. It must have been difficult for him working in Scotland during the War but he never sought approval or popularity from the pupils.

"Stand up Douglas, and read out your Latin translation."

I stood up at my desk in the front row and stumbled over the first sentences.

"That's enough," Fritz roared, "You obviously haven't done your homework, come out here."

Down came the tawse, as if he was representing the German army in the enemy classroom. Roy, the boy next to me was visibly shaking. His attempt at the translation was no better than mine and Fritz opened his desk again. Roy was an only child, his father was in the forces and I don't think he had received the belt in his short life, but Fritz had no favourites. Even the girls were regularly belted. The crack sent a shudder right through the classroom, and Roy walked slowly back to his seat and sat down. The next moment another resounding crack vibrated round the hushed room.

Roy had fainted and knocked his head on the wooden floor. I leaned over and dragged him to an upright position where he sat ashen faced.

"The fool must be delicate," Fritz muttered.

Roy, alone in the class, was never belted by Fritz again but given lines instead. He was a very good scholar, except for languages, and a fine athlete. He got on well with all the teachers except Fritz. I think he must have fainted from sheer shock. Even the other teachers were overawed by Fritz. Another boy and I were kept behind to put away mats after a PT period.

"Tell Mr. Deicher that I'm sorry for keeping you back," the gym teacher said.

Fritz refused to listen to our explanation and reached in his desk for the well worn piece of leather. We complained later to the Gym Teacher and he exclaimed, "Oh I must apologise to Mr. Deicher when I see him."

Last period on a Tuesday was for preparation, and a grim faced teacher of mathematics discovered that I was missing. The sun was shining, the sky was blue and the Gairney had called me to her waters. I was sent for on Wednesday morning.

"Where were you last period yesterday?" he thundered.

"Please Sir, I felt sick and had to go home."

"Fetch me a note from your mother tomorrow," he retorted.

Like the fish I had lost at the Gairney, I felt that I had been let off the hook. Mother, however, refused to help me out. "You'll just have to tell the truth and take your punishment."

There was nothing else for it. I wrote the note myself trying to copy Mother's large sprawling handwriting. The teacher put on his spectacles and examined it carefully.

"Fetch me a copy of your own handwriting," he said quietly and ominously. He studied the two scraps of paper side by side, folded them up and put them in his wallet. I sat in suspense for a week waiting for a summons to the headmaster's office. Nothing happened and I breathed easily again. Thank goodness it hadn't been Fritz in charge of preparation. As it was, the week's waiting had been an effective punishment on its own.

The subjects I liked at school were few. English, I loved. We read Shakespeare and acted some of the plays. I remember being given the part of Julius Ceasar, stabbed in the back with a ruler and rolling down three wooden steps, to the applause of the class. I was in my natural element in the gymnasium, of course, and represented the school in athletics.

The only other subject that I enjoyed was Art. The room was so quiet and relaxed after the tension and frustration of more taxing subjects. There were some marvellous stuffed birds and I particularly liked drawing a heron with its long spindly legs and rapier beak.

Fortunately no stuffed jackdaw adorned the Art room or I might not have been so enthusiastic about drawing birds. The Art teacher puffed away at his pipe sometimes at the back of the room and drank coffee in the small staff room every hour or so. He told us he loved painting gypsies and at one time considered giving up his job and travelling the country in a horse drawn caravan. It all sounded so romantic, artist and gypsy combined. That's the life for me, I thought. I left school at fourteen, glad to escape from the tyranny, with not even one certificate to show that I had completed nine years of study.

I wasn't very well equipped to start an apprenticeship in building. The other apprentices had all done Technical subjects at school and were proficient in woodwork and metalwork while I had spent two years wrestling with Latin and French taught by a German teacher.

Hair lice were very common at the school and, as my three sisters had long hair, Mother had a job keeping them clean. Each evening she sat at the fireside with a big metal tray and a bone comb. The girls knelt down in front of her in turn and Mother vigorously combed their hair, the girls yelling occasionally as the comb stuck at the tuggy bits.

I appointed myself chief executioner and as the tiny white struggling nits fell onto the tray, pressed them with my thumb nail, delighting in the sharp satisfying crack. The girls were lucky. My hair care was the responsibility of Father. He insisted on cutting my hair on the front lawn and performed the ritual with great style. I sat on a wooden chair and he tied a white tablecloth round my neck with a fine flourish. He moved around me as graceful as a matador in spite of his bad leg, snip, snip, snipping with scissors and comb, locks of hair floating about like feathers from a hen being plucked. He was well equipped with a little brown varnished box filled with various sizes of clippers, combs and scissors. Some of the clippers were blunt and I winced occasionally as little tufts were pulled out of my neck.

"Oh, that's sair."

"Ah dinny ken hoo yir sae sensitive," he grumbled. "The men it ma work dinny complain when ah cut thir hair."

Probably the low price he charged kept them passive. A small crowd of the curious would gather as he performed his barbaric barbery and this encouraged him to more extravagant flourishes, an ear would be nicked only to be swabbed with a small piece of cotton wool from the magical box. Father smoked as he worked and ash would drop occasionally on to my neck to add to my discomfort. He always finished with the same final remark.

"There, yi could pey wan and six it the barbers, and it widnae be half as guid a hair cut is that."

When I did go the barber occasionally I'm sure he felt betrayed and was very critical.

"Hoo much did ye pey fir that? He's no made a very guid job o it. He's geed ye a can can," and so on.

He always insisted that I swept up the lawn afterwards. This I didn't mind. There was something fascinating about the act. The large nest of hair feeling part of you yet slightly removed. I suppose a stag must feel the same way when it casts its antlers or a snake its old skin.

Father was very good with his hands. He mended everything requiring mending, lawn mowers, taps, roller skates, fences, the lot. He had a cobbler's last with the various iron fittings and mended all our shoes, cutting down old footwear for the best scraps of leather. We were always well shod. Bikes were Dad's speciality and he would dismantle and re-assemble the intricate three speed gear mechanism. He saved up parts of old bikes to rebuild them into one machine. He worked for a long time on a bike for me and at last it was completed except for the brake blocks.

"You'll hae tae wait till ah git intae Cowdenbeath fir a new set."

I pleaded with him for a shot. Against his better judgement, he relented.

"Ye kin hae a shot along that cul-de-sac where it's level, bit go dead slow in mind - dinny go near that main road."

I obeyed his instructions for a while, it was great having my own bike at last.

"Come oan wi me fir a message," Jackie shouted.

I decided to accompany him but, unwilling to part with my bike, decided to push it. This became tedious after a while and I hit on an idea.

"You sit on the seat, Jackie, and ah'll sit oan the crossbar. Yi kin brake the back wheel wi yir fit, and ah'll dae the same wi the front wan."

We started off slowly and cautiously but the bike gathered momentum and we lost control. The brae was very steep and we were heading for Kelty Cross. Jackie and I started to roar for help. The bike was now going too fast to jump off. A long line of miners were walking up the brae, just finished the dayshift. Spike, a giant of a man, jumped onto the road and stood, waiting, legs apart, as solid as a rock. As soon as we reached him he grabbed the handlebars and stopped the bike dead. Jackie and I flew past him and somersaulted onto the road. Spike inspected us anxiously. We were lucky, with only a few minor cuts and bruises. The news reached my father before I arrived home and he stood in the living room grim faced. Without a word he pointed to the side of an arm chair and started to unbuckle his leather belt.

My eldest sister Ellen was unlucky in some ways as a child. She decided to do some housework one day when Mother was out shopping and put on a large apron much too big for her. After tidying up the fireplace she started to dust the mantelpiece. The apron caught fire and she rushed to the door in panic, luckily changing her mind then running back to the bathroom. She jumped in the bath and I helped to splash water to put out the flames.

One leg had a severe burn and Mother was very upset when she arrived home, blaming herself for leaving us on our own. Shortly afterwards, Ellen had pleurisy. When I was at school, tuberculosis was still fairly rife in the village. Due to overcrowded conditions whole families would be affected by the disease and we lost several of our school friends. Ellen was suspected of having the disease and the doctor sent her to the Lomond Hills Sanatorium for a few weeks and they finally decided that she didn't have tuberculosis and sent her home.

When she was taken to the Sanatorium, only Mother was allowed to visit her, to keep contact to a minimum. One day I was determined to see my sister and followed Mother down the street like an untrained puppy, stopping when she stopped and walking when she walked. She hadn't time to take me home and reluctantly decided that I could accompany her. At the Sanatorium, Mother left me at a determined spot from the big iron gates while she went inside.

After a while she brought Ellen near to the gates and we waved to each other. I wanted to approach closer but Mother shouted me back. I couldn't see anything dangerous but recognised the anxiety in Mother's voice and half expected to see a mad patient rushing at me and rattling at the iron gates. I didn't know how the disease affected them. Gradually treatment improved and TB was no longer a scourge in the village.

I fell in love for the first time. A circus arrived in the village and parked in a field beside the Black Burn, only a hundred yards from our house. It must have been an offshoot of a larger circus as there was only a big tent, several caravans, one elephant, a few small cages of animals and six or so performers who seemed to have an amazing variety of roles.

The man selling tickets at the entrance appeared in a strong man act later on in the evening, while an usherette did a dramatic switch to animal trainer. The owner's daughter, Rosita, was sent to our school for the fortnight the circus was in Kelty. Her education must have been built up from snatches of information from many of the small villages of the land. She was small, gypsy looking with dark, knowing eyes and white teeth, and I thought she was the prettiest girl that I had ever seen.

Rosita only spoke a few words to me in the fortnight but that only added to her mystique. I hung about the circus in the evening like a hungry dog catching only an occasional glimpse of Rosita as she went about her chores. She was wonderfully aloof and unattainable. I had protested when Mother asked me to collect horse manure from the street and here was this small girl, shovel in hand, responsible for the wellbeing and cleanliness of an elephant.

Everything had to be seen in the right proportion, even dung. Yes, she was wonderful. I did a few handsprings and cartwheels in sight of her father, hoping that he would see my potential as an acrobat and offer to take me with him but he seemed indifferent. Soon the glamour and excitement moved on and only a circle of flattened grass and a torn gaudy poster stuck forlornly on a twig reminded me of dark-eyed Rosita who first awakened the pangs of unrequited love.

DOOHILL CASTLE

During the summer holidays, Mother always took us to Dowhill Castle, a ruin about four miles from Kelty near the Cleish Crags. We were allowed a friend each, so that made eight children altogether. Other children heard of the outing and asked to come along, so in a space of a few years the eight grew to an average of twenty. Mother, a dynamic five foot tall leader and unofficial social worker handled them all easily. The children would do anything for her, even the toughest of boys. She even tried to like Pud, who came occasionally. I don't know if she succeeded but Mother never admitted failure. We set off happy and excited, two boy cousins from Perth with us, loving the countryside after the city. All the children carried something to eat and Mother always had extra sandwiches and lemonade. No one went hungry on her picnics.

The route led past Blairadam Big House. Mother had permission to take the children through the estate and they behaved well, keeping to the path. We passed Kiery Craigs Lodge, North Blair and sank down gratefully at Dichendad for a rest. Everyone had a tinful of iron water to fortify them for the rest of the journey and a shoot of rhubarb growing in a ruined garden nearby. We moved on past Sunnyside and Flockhouse then the castle came into view on top of a hill and everyone gave a cry of relief.

The castle was very exciting with dungeons below, dark and mysterious and on the first floor little bowers to sit with a marvellous view over the countryside. There was no roof on the castle so it was very pleasant high up. One wall was very steep and dangerous, the opposite tumbling away gradually. The children swarmed all over the area, the castle itself, a round tower, and large rhododendron bushes like great tents once you climbed inside. There were rabbits galore to be chased, nests to be explored and occasional glimpses of pheasants, owls and roe deer. Mother called to us all for the picnic and we squatted on the castle like knights of old having a banquet. Loch Leven could be seen a few miles away, and there was a legend that an underground tunnel linked Dowhill with the castle on an island in the Loch.

A narrow crevice above the stone bower caught Jackie's eye. He jumped up and discovered a colony of bats. We gave him a long stick and he poked them out. They chattered in a high pitch, perhaps ten or so, and fluttered above us wildly for a few seconds, then flew in a group to the peace of some dark trees. Funny little things, half bird and half mouse in a way slightly awesome even in the daylight, due to their connection in our minds with Count Dracula.

A rabbit rose suddenly from behind a stone and a Perth cousin gave chase, running right over the parapet and falling about six feet. Luckily it wasn't the steep wall or he would never have chased another rabbit again.

It was time to go. The sun had gone down, the air was chillier and some of the younger children were glancing apprehensively at the sky in case the bats were returning to their roosting place. We set off on the long walk home.

Even after we grew up, Mother still took crowds of children to the castle. After she became too frail for the walk she hired a bus to carry on the tradition. The picnic ceased when it poured buckets of rain one day, few turned up and Mother had to meet most of the cost herself.

Dunfermline was five miles away and had the nearest swimming pool. We went occasionally when our parents gave us our fare and entry money but we nearly all learned to swim in the Black Burn. The boys piled up divots and stones at a wide part of the burn. The water was already dark, flowing from the peaty Loch Glow and the divots made it darker still. It was more like swimming in tea than water. The floor would be very uneven with large stones, pebbles and mud. One step and you could descend from the knees to the waist. The bigger boys were very good, holding up your chin while you kicked out at the breast stroke and most of us learned quickly.

Jackie and I carried our medical supplies. He had his sticking plaster and I carried a small bottle of Dettol. I was allergic to insect bites and the affected limb would swell up alarmingly. The clegs or horse flies were the biggest menace of The Dookie. They were big insects yet you never felt them landing. The sudden bite made me shudder and I would squash the fly in a panic, the damage already done. If I applied Dettol straight away, the swelling wasn't so bad. One big boy didn't seem to be affected at all. He would deliberately allow the cleg to drink its fill then squash it against his arm, the blood squirting out like the water from a pistol.

If I got stung by a wasp I would be ill and in bed for one or two days. I remember being stung on the head by a large bee and running screaming to Mother. She picked out the sting with a pair of tweezers and placed it on the polished table where it spun round and round like a top, the nerve still active. A tree stood beside the Dookie and some boys had fixed a thick rope to a branch. We took turn each at swinging high, letting go at the apex and splashing into the water below.

The water got even blacker still and with all the mud started to look more like treacle than tea. No one tried swimming under water. Even the fish wore miners' lamps in the Black Burn, Craw used to say. It must have been very unhealthy in the Dookie with drains running from the village and fields but we never gave it a thought - until one occasion.

Jackie and I walked over one morning when it was just starting to get warm. There was no one else there and we undressed quickly wanting to be first in. A nasty odour hung about the air and we hesitated on the bank trying to trace the source. Jackie groaned suddenly and pointing to the dam said, "There'll be nae swimmin the day."

A dead sheep had been washed down and lay jammed between two big stones.

TATTIE HOWKIN

Mother woke us up in the dark mornings. We were very reluctant to rise. The beds were warm, safe cocoons and the air in the rooms cold.

"C'mon, up ye get, " Mother said, "Yir breakfast's ready."

We stumbled, heavy eyed to the living room where a big fire burned, and scrambled eggs on toast lay on a table. It was still dark when the lorry arrived in the street and the tattie howkers piled in. Bundles of straw had been flung on the floor and acted as shock absorbers from the bumping of the lorry. The fields under the Cleish Crags lay still and uninviting; even the creatures of the wild didn't seem to be up and about yet. This was the worst time of the day, the first stint to be picked, the first bending of a stiff back and lifting a heavy basket of potatoes. After that it wasn't quite so bad.

Everyone thought that the farmer or his foreman had misjudged the stints marked out with branches stuck into the ground and each worker paced his own out again comparing it to his immediate neighbour's, unwilling to believe that theirs wasn't a bit longer than anyone else's. If, by some misfortune, you landed next to Pud, of course, the chances were that yours would be a bit more and his a bit less. The tractor had no sooner passed, the potatoes lifted, than it seemed to be on you again. As we lay flat out, resting between the drills it looked like a malevolent robot bearing down, programmed to go round and round the field for ever.

If you lay still you were finished, no way was that metal monster going to stop, unless an extra large stone or a boggy patch halted its progress for an all too brief spell. When that happened, a great cheer arose from the workers enjoying a slightly longer break. When the whistle went for piece time it sounded sweeter than the blackie or the thrush.

"That can't be the tractor starting up again," Craw moaned, "We've only had five minutes."

But alas it was, clanging, rattling, snorting, our mechanical task master. The man on top seemed anonymous, part of the machine, never exchanging greetings with us like the more human carters. Perhaps he, too, thought he was condemned to go round and round forever.

The digger disturbed a lot of animals. Field mice and voles would be unearthed and before they had time to recover from the shock the boys would grab them ignoring the bites, sometimes in their eagerness, grasping too tightly, until some poor rodent's eyes seemed to pop out further than Nature intended. A rabbit was a great prize. Sometimes one would lie between the drills hiding in the grass and potato shaws, then dashed madly when disturbed. The panic stricken animal would be chased all over the field until it either escaped or took refuge in a dry stane dyke or burrow.

If the burrow was shallow one boy would lie face down wards on the ground and stretch an arm to grasp the rabbit, which would be dragged out, struggling and kicking violently. It would be held by the ears and given a quick chop, appropriately called a rabbit punch to the side of the neck, A favourite girl friend was often nonchalantly tossed the rabbit as the hunters of old dropped the carcase of wild animals on the cave floor. Only the language was different.

"Me mighty hunter, kill great bear." "Here hen, here's a rabbit fir ye."

The mole was the strangest animal to be unearthed, helpless and blinded by the light at first, and the object of the most curiosity, with pink nose and long whiskers quivering, great hands held sideways like a priest offering a prayer. As soon as they realised their predicament the moles burrowed furiously, shovelling the earth backwards and disappearing from sight in seconds as if the earth had swallowed them whole. The moles were never harmed, perhaps miners' sons recognising an affinity with their fathers' lives.

Tattie howkin was an immoral time, inhibitions falling like fragile leaves in the rude, raw existence of the fields. Bawdy songs were sung in the lorry with great gusto. No deference was paid to the girls. It was as if they had lost the privileges of the female sex as soon as they abandoned their own clothes and wore the same as the boys, dungarees, jerseys, bonnets and boots or wellingtons.

Some of the bolder children succumbed quickly to the earthier atmosphere of farm life and all sorts of liaisons sprung up. The men who worked on the farm encouraged the crudity. They had always been closer to nature. Boy meets girl seemed to be the same to them as bull meets cow or boar meets sow. Some of the women who came to work on the farm were a very rough lot too. Rodney, a big boy of sixteen who was staying on at school to be educated and spoke very properly, was very condescending to them, saying, "I'm not used to such rough talk at home."

Several women descended on him like locusts and, from the flurry of bodies, flew a pair of trousers followed closely by a pair of underpants. The watching crowd cheered and laughed, some of the boys a trifle nervously, perhaps wondering if they would be next.

Rodney's speech roughened noticeably as the days went on. Tattie howkin was a dehumanising existence. Clothes were not washed until the end of the tattie holidays so every day clothes stiff with sweat and dirt had to be put on. Finger nails became broken and filthy, faces weather beaten and lips chapped. Walking upright became a problem after work, the back more used to the horizontal position like the beasts of the field.

When Mother came with us things improved slightly. She tried to keep the girl workers under her wings like a mother hen. No rude songs were sung in the lorry when she was there. She even persuaded the children to sing hymns occasionally. She loved children and knew them all by their first names. They appreciated this and treated her with respect and affection.

She arranged with the farmer for a corner of the farmyard to be reserved for the girls' toilets, away from the prying eyes of the boys. Lunch time was always the best part of the day, a whole hour to eat sandwiches then roam the farmyard. Most of the farmers allowed us to wander about at will. We jumped and rolled in the hay lofts, swung on the rafters and sampled the treacle from the big barrel in the cowshed.

The hens must have dreaded this annual invasion. A hand was often roughly shoved under an outraged bird and her egg removed. The hens nested all over the farmyard, not just in the hen sheds, and their hidey holes were eagerly sought out by the boys. The farmer wrote off his eggs as natural losses, as he ignored the small bags of potatoes furtively carried on to the lorry at finishing time. Mother banned her own children from any of these practices but the farmer knew her principles well and a large bag of potatoes would appear at the end of the holidays on our doorstep.

On a good day the work was tolerable. We climbed onto the bogey once to be taken to a field lying under Cleish Crags. The tractor chugged up a leafy lane and the workers laughed, joked and jostled in the bogey. Branches brushed our faces and, at the back of the bogey, Craw, the city boy, grabbed one in delight, feeling the rough texture of the bark and the smooth silkiness of the leaves. But he forgot to let go, lost his balance and was left dangling like a puppet on a string high above the ground. The Cleish Crags loomed on the horizon and at our approach hundreds of jackdaws filled the air with their clamour.

It was a warm day for a change and we worked in our shirt sleeves. About lunch time we ran out of baskets and were forced to make piles of potatoes at the side of our stints. This was extra work so the word passed from mouth to mouth. 'Strike.' Tattie howkers in my day seemed to strike often. I suppose that in a mining area they tended to be militant and any excuse was a break in the monotony. Bob, the farmer, arrived very flustered and after promising more baskets the following day we all trooped back to work.

One farmer at Abernethy really enraged the workers. He paid the oldest children who were doing the same work as adults, three quarter stints. Half stints were common for young children but three quarters unheard of. We worked a week there then left. Some children were always being lured by extra money and would leave to join

another squad. The wages varied from ten shillings to twelve and six a day. The farmers who paid the most worked you the hardest. There was nothing for nothing.

Towards the end of the tattie holidays, I resolved to try to tame a bank vole. Just before stopping time the digger unearthed a young one and I put him struggling into a jam jar filled with grass. The lorry rattled and rumbled all the way home as usual, sore on our aching bodies. In the house I anxiously took the lid of the jar and lifted out the vole, placing it on the floor to see if it was alright. To the family's amusement, the tiny rodent shook violently in the same rhythm as the vibrating lorry for several minutes, much as a sailor walks with a rolling gait when on dry land. When the shaking stopped for some reason the vole was perfectly tame, started sniffing around, and accepted a blade of grass from me. It sat on its hind legs like a beaver, held the grass in its front paw and nibbled away. In a short time it was coming voluntarily over to me and accepting food.

This was amazing, a wild creature from the fields, its first time in a house, showing no fear. Perhaps the jolting lorry had performed some sort of brain washing or bashing. Wait till I showed the vole to Jackie and Craw. Me, their friend, Doctor Doolittle of the tattie-fields, able to tame wild animals. Many a bite they had received from bank voles. I played with my new pet until bedtime then Father put it in a deep tin for the night so that it couldn't jump out.

Dan the cat was showing interest, but not too much. For added safety Father put the tin on top of the book-case, placing a book as a cover. He and mother slept in the big bed in the living room at the time and, putting out the light, they climbed into bed. The room was still lit by firelight. Dan lay sleeping peacefully on the rug. All was still. The vole rustled the straw in the tin.

Quick as a flash Dan sprang on to the book case, knocked off the book and scooped out the vole. Father hopped clumsily out of bed but too late to save the small trusting creature. In the morning I woke early and came rushing through to see my new pet only to be told the sad news by Mother.

"A cat can't help its nature, son," she said.

I tried to help Dan's nature by giving him a hard smack.

He must have been puzzled, thinking no doubt that he was usually applauded for catching a mouse in the home.

Jim and Ellen

THE CINEMA

The village had two cinemas, the Gothenburg and the Regal. They each changed their programme three times a week so that it was possible to see a different film each night apart from Sunday. One woman in the village was an addict and could be seen near the head of the queue every night. You could also of course see two films the same evening as there were two sessions, six to eight and eight to ten.

My sisters and I were given tuppence for the matinee on Saturday afternoon. The serials were good, with Flash Gordon and The Clutching Hand among others. Inevitably the older Cinema, The Gothenburg, was called the Flea Pit. It had very old upholstered seats and a lodger could become very attached to you during the programme. At the Goth, the curtains looked tremendous when lit up, the colours changing with the slightest movement. When the lights went up and the film started, cheers and cat calls filled the air. There seemed to be always someone changing their seats as liaisons took place between the boys and girls. Scuffles broke out frequently and the usherette would suddenly shine a torch and some miscreant would be ejected.

Occasionally the manager would be called as some unwilling boy had to be persuaded to leave. Some courting couples received fame in the village by being banned from both the Goth and the Regal, perhaps for life. We never heard of anyone being let in again, the torrid love scenes had only to take place on the screen.

The projector light was fascinating in the darkness as it constantly changed its tone working at the screen. Some of the bolder spirits threw up pieces of silver paper and these twinkled like stars instant before falling. The most dangerous seats in the cinema were under the balcony. In the darkness cigarette ends, apple runts and other missiles would descend with sudden shock on the recipients below.

After all the fun, glamour and excitement of the programme, what a difference when the lights went on at the close. The place had a musty sweaty odour, the curtains looked faded and dowdy, litter lay everywhere and you were in danger of being crushed as the crowds jostled and fought to get out.

Occasionally father took us through the week as a special treat. This was much better than the matinee as the children were controlled by their parents and thus there was a more peaceful and relaxing atmosphere. The only real noise came when the projector broke down and after ten minutes or so, some of the audience would stamp their feet with impatience. The manager would appear on the stage and ask for volunteers to sing for a pound each. Half a dozen amateur artistes would entertain us well until the film came on again.

As children we loved the horror films, often lying awake at night afterwards in terror. On one occasion, I received some money from an uncle and went to the cinema at night. The film was 'The Wolfman,' with Lon Chaney and was very frightening. In one scene he sits in his room watching hair growing thicker and thicker on his arms and in another he prowls about in dark trees in the moonlight. It was winter and the snow lay about a foot thick. When I came out I decided to take a short cut over the fields to home. I wasn't apprehensive as I started out, but gradually became aware that the clump of trees on my left, with the clouds scudding over the moon, was very similar to a scene in the film. I glanced fearfully over my shoulder and was shocked to see a tall dark figure following me. A dog mourned to the moon nearby and I was gripped with panic. I started to walk faster but the snow impeded my wellington boots. I couldn't run, just kept pushing against the white barrier.

The figure was gaining and I thought "This is it, the Wolfman has got me."

A familiar voice shattered the icy air. "Tak yir time."

It was Jock Gray, a boy who lived near me. I nearly collapsed into the snow with relief.

"Ah've been tryin tae catch up wi ye since ye came oot the pickchur hoose. A didnae want tae cross the field massel efter that scary film."

We ploughed on together happy and confident. Two of us were a match for any werewolf.

An old man across the road from us came in frequently for a meal for a while. His wife had died and as he was lonely Mother asked him over. He really appreciated this and gave the children gifts, some things he had kept for years. I got a very good projector and some old films. Friends and my sisters would crowd our bedroom for a film show. There was no screen so the projector would be focussed on a wall. The other thing missing was a container for the light bulb, which had to be a two hundred and fifty watt or so, and I made one out of a dried milk tin with a hole punched in one end for the light and a hole in the lid for the cable.

How someone didn't get electrocuted I don't know. The tin would become unbearably hot and Jackie or Craw would hold it with a wet cloth to keep it cool, while the steam rose from the tin. I turned the handle by hand quickly. We stopped from time to time to allow the tin to cool down and, on putting on the light, would often discover yards and yards of film on the floor. All this added to the fun and the audience thought these shows tremendous. One of my friends was an apprentice operator in the

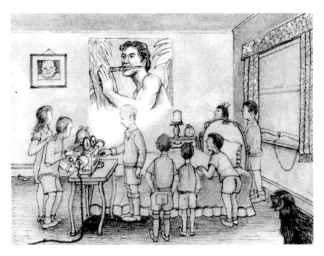

Gothenburg and he gave me a load of cuttings from the feature films.

On the bedroom wall we were then able to show stills of great stars, sometimes, their heads much bigger than life size. It seemed a great achievement in a small bedroom watching Tarzan of the Apes gaze down from the trees above the bed.

KELTY KLONDYKE

One summer, a miniature Klondyke started in the quarry. A man digging for
docken grubs discovered a long seam of coal very close to the surface. The quarry was,
of course, already a deep depression in the ground, scooped to supply clay for
Blairadam Brickworks. Officialdom closed a blind eye for a while. The miners had
free coal but other workers in the village did not have this concession. They descended
like wasps to a jam jar, men, women and children with all sorts of improvised barrows,
some wood, some metal, and old prams. They dug with spades, picks, shovels, hoes,
gardening forks, filling bag after bag. It was summer and the ice cream van did a
roaring trade nearby.

The seam was at a slight angle and was soon stripped near the surface. As the top
coal was cleared, they started digging tunnels. Feet could be seen sticking out of a
hole, kicking vigorously in effort, earth flying, in fact, much like a dog digging for a
rabbit. Old fence posts were pulled out of the ground to be used as props. The tunnel
got deeper, some of the smaller barrows were pushed in and filled at the coal face.
Inevitably, someone was going to get killed if the work carried on, and also some
enterprising men and boys were selling bags of coal in the village at cut prices.

The police arrived with large notices pertaining to tresspassing and fines, and
council workmen filled in the holes. The amateur miners departed, apart from the
bolder spirits going on the night shift with a pick and a torch at a spot hidden from the
road. The coal rush was over but many families were stocked up for the winter. A
similar incident occurred, in a minor way, when construction started on the motorway
at the top end of the village years later.

A monster walked into the village one day. She was awesome, higher than the
highest house, snorting, grunting, belching black smoke, eyes flashing, flattening
bushes, fences and hedges, leaving her claw marks over miles of countryside. She was
first seen moving jerkily round the side of Benarty Hill, cows and sheep running away
in alarm. When she crossed a road it broke into fragments under the enormous weight.
Her neck was long with a large open mouth and teeth a yard long. She seemed
harmless to humans as long as they didn't get too near. If they did, a surprisingly thin
human-like voice whined above the noise.

"Get back, get back."

The villagers called her Mona. She was really a Monican crane heading for
Cocklaw Farm to commence opencast mining.

I suppose that the route chosen for the journey offered the least possible damage
but the moving tracks devastated fields, especially where the ground was soft. It had to
cross some roads, and men and equipment stood by to repair the damage as soon as the
monster passed. Before Mona arrived at the village, people walked for miles to see her.
It became a family outing, a picnic with lemonade and sandwiches. Arriving at her
destination Mona swung into action, with her bulldozers in attendance. The ground
was scraped and shovelled into piles revealing the coal underneath.

The crane worked night and day, lights flashing, clanging and groaning, the noise terrific. The former peaceful grazing fields world turned into a nightmarish scene, like no man's land in the first war, large mounds of earth and mud, pools of stagnant water, broken posts sticking up like accusing fingers, dead, bare trees, debris and oil drums. Blasting went on constantly, the villagers receiving notices of the denoted times. The seams of coal revealed were astounding. Kelty was sitting on a great coal cellar stretching for miles. As soon as the crane moved on a bit the boys moved in. This was a new playground, with trees leaning at peculiar angles, steep bings to slide down, stones and pebbles to throw in the pools. Pieces of strum, explosive cord, were discovered and these were greatly prized.

We spent a long time carefully unravelling the outer casing to reach the powder at the centre. We made bangers out of two six inch bolts held together at the center with a nut. Some powder was put in and the bolts tightened up. When flung at a wall or dropped on the pavement they gave a tremendous bang, wisps of smoke emerging and the strong smell of cordite in the air. This was much better than the match heads we used normally.

Then one day Mona moved on, towering above the trees like some prehistoric animal, the earth robbed of its treasure. The bulldozers certainly made a good job of rehabilitating the lands. The fields were flattened and rolled, replanted with grass and the cows returned from their exile in strange fields to graze peacefully again in Kelty.

A mining village was a warm friendly place but like other villages had its share of prowlers and perverts. The children knew the men to avoid in the woods and for the most part they were harmless peeping toms, students in the art of courting, by proxy. A few were dangerous. Tammy Tickler, as he was known, a tall man with small appraising eyes and a slack smile always wanted to teach the boys wrestling.

"Aye it's done me in good stead aw ma life, Yi nivver ken when somewan's gonny set on ye," he would say, but any real interest in the sport was suspect. Some of the older, bolder boys told stories of his collection of wrestling photographs in his house where any resemblance to a noble art was difficult to find. Our little group kept well out of his way.

On a nesting outing, Craw and I were crawling through undergrowth in the spruce woods of the Forestry Commission. It was starting to get dark as we neared the road and a small clearing was a welcome respite. We were startled by a dark figure standing close to the trunk of a tree. He looked vaguely familiar but had his collar up and bunnet pulled well down. I was nearly sure it was Arthur Erskine. Craw and I were poised to run when he spoke.

"Dinna be feared, boys," he said softly, "Wid ye dae a message fir me?"

We didn't answer.

"Di ye ken Mrs. Jenkins, she's a lodger wi auld Tamson?"

We nodded.

"Ah'll gie ye threepence each if ye tak her this note".

I noticed for the first time that he held a small cairn terrier in his arms. Craw stretched a grubby hand forward, not getting too close while I stood still, ready to run for help if he was grabbed. We ran from the woods, relieved to see the friendly lights of the village.

Mrs. Jenkins was an English woman who had recently arrived in the village. Old Tamson, sensing a drama came hobbling through to the scullery. For some reason she read the note out loud 'If you want your dog back, come to the Lochornie Bridge. If you come, come alone.'

Old Tamson became very agitated. "Tak nothing tae dae wi it. Send the laddies doon tae the polis station."

"No, no," Mrs Jenkins said, " think I know who it is and if I don't meet him, I'll never get my Perky back."

It was all too complicated for Craw and me, just another example of the puzzling world of adults. It was easier to know what a frog or a rabbit was thinking. Mrs. Jenkins gave us another threepence each and we felt she was a fine woman. We bought chips with the money feeling sorrier for the small dog than for any of the adult participants.

I passed Arthur Erskine the following day and he avoided my stare but he usually did any way. Arthur was funny, no doubt about that. Since he hung his socks on her girdle, Miss Knight thought so too, and little presents came popping through her letter box at night; a box of soap, a rose. Perhaps it was senility but he couldn't be that old, fifty or so.

His wife, Sarah, was a small, thin, dusky, beetle-like woman, with short black hair and thick spectacles, the opposite really of Miss Knight, who was big, fair and buxom.

Sarah considered Arthur handsome, thinking the heavy jaw strong, the secret smile, good humour and the childish blue eyes appealing. She knew that she was lucky to have won him, but there were always malicious neighbours ready to whisper stories. After all when he chopped down the monkey puzzle tree in the front garden he wasn't to know it would fall the wrong way and block the road for a morning. When Miss Knight complained that her water was giving her trouble, hardly a dribble, Arthur managed to adjust the main so that she had all the water she could use even though the rest of the street diminished to a trickle. It was a bit embarrassing, certainly, that Miss Knight was in when Arthur arrived home from the backshift. He just stripped off quickly and got into the tub before they had time to move to the scullery. Miss Knight wasn't married of course or she wouldn't have been so shocked. Arthur was a good man really, always giving her a hand about the house and insisting on hanging up the washing, a job he really seemed to enjoy.

Between them they had produced one daughter, Irene. She was a beautiful girl, tall, slim, graceful, with long black hair. It's a pity she was a snob. Irene went for music lessons, but plenty of people played the fiddle. Even in our street Henry played the fiddle, wee Erchie played the fiddle and the melodeon. But Irene called her fiddle a violin. It's funny how it changed names when you took music lessons. I rather liked her myself, but what a father.

In spite of all the misdemeanours of some of the villagers, very seldom were the police called in. They represented authority, and miners disliked authority. Apart from

that most families had skeletons in their own closets and were reluctant to point an accusing finger at a neighbour. After coming out of the Boys' Club at night we were sometimes served by a dour, uncommunicative man in the fish and chip shop nearby. They said he had been in a concentration camp before being demobbed.

In spite of several warnings, children ruffled through the pile of cut newspapers kept for wrapping up the chips. The man would struggle to control his anger while beads of sweat gathered on his brow. His hands shook noticeably. Suddenly he lifted the big potato slicing knife and brought it down crashing on to the wooden counter, inches from the culprits' fingers, nearly turning them into chips. No one ever reported him, to my knowledge. The village was very tolerant and though he didn't like children, he certainly knew how to get the best out of a haddock.

JAKE

Jake grew into a beautiful bird, glossy feathers, swaggering gait, eyes bluer and wickeder than ever. He followed me everywhere. When I dug for worms for the fishing he got in the road of the spade and risked his life, nearly being guillotined once or twice as he picked the choicest worms and grubs for himself. He was more independent now, not coming immediately to my call, but, like a disobedient child, taking his own time, flying to me eventually, if sometimes reluctantly. Wild jackdaws hung about the chimneys of Braewell and Jake had contacted them, the wild birds often retreating from his advances, no doubt astonished that this bold fellow actually consorted with humans. When I cycled he flew over the bike adjusting his speed perfectly, resting on my head or shoulders whenever he felt like it.

Jake was kept in the shed all day for safety when I was at school, but given his freedom in the evenings and weekends. A window was kept open in the house for him and he entered and left as he pleased. He often fell asleep at night perched on top of a wooden chair until I arrived home and took him to the shed. He could have lived easily as one of the family except for his habit of excreting without warning so that his visits to the living room were curtailed. A chimpanzee can be fitted with a nappy but this would look grotesque on a jackdaw. If only he could have been house trained! Jake seemed to like sweet tea. If any was left in a cup he would fly to the table, dip his beak, suck some up then lifting his beak upwards swallowed noisily with great satisfaction. If he was given a piece of cheese he would fly quickly away as if it was a treasure and became very agitated if any one came near him while he was pecking furiously at it. My sisters admired him but never allowed him to perch on their arms, his toilet habits being too erratic for them.

Father was quietly pleased that I was following in his footsteps and relished his role as wild life adviser. As with all pets, Mother showed little interest but tolerated them for our sakes. Human beings were her forte and her great natural affection didn't seem to extend to the animal kingdom.

A bath was a great treat for Jake. I half filled a shallow basin with water and he hopped in, flapping his wings in delight, sprinkling water all over his body, mouth agape as if he was gasping for air. He could never make up his mind when he was finished, coming out for a few minutes, shaking the water off vigorously, then, changing his mind, in again for more. When his feathers got wet he seemed to shrink in size, his neck incredibly scrawny and his belly once more becoming bare. Often I had to empty the basin or he would have bathed for hours. After his bath he perched on the fence and preened himself all over, sifting feathers through his beak methodically.

Still damp, he strutted about the garden looking as foolish as a hen. When I held him on a wrist he was fascinated by my teeth and he picked in the spaces between them finding tiny particles of food which he chewed with great relish, perhaps another echo of his past when one of his parents disgorged food for him. I always felt apprehensive when that sharp beak was too close to my eyes, though not once did he attempt to peck at them. Sometimes when he found a particularly choice morsel in my teeth, he became quite excited and started to hammer away like a demented woodpecker until stopped. When sitting on my shoulder he loved to pull at my ear lobes and sift through my hair with the same attention he gave his feathers.

"He's just like Mum wi the bone comb," my younger sister observed.

I never felt secure when Jake sat on top of my head, feeling too vulnerable to his excretory indiscretions. His manners were appalling, really. Jake had to be rescued on several occasions. Once he stuck his head through a piece of wire netting and nearly strangled himself pulling to get out. Another time he landed in a water barrel at the end of Father's greenhouse, thinking, no doubt, that it was a giant bath. When I arrived only his head was above the surface. He squawked weakly at me in faint recognition and nearly went under as his mouth took in water.

Jake puzzled our cat and dog. They expected birds to fly from them but Jake landed confidently on their backs and when they ran in ancestral fright, thinking perhaps he was an eagle, he stayed on for a while, flapping his wings to keep balance and gripping hard on his furry mounts. It's always difficult to know if pets recognise other pets and feel inhibited about harming them. Our cat killed dozens of birds, usually quickly and methodically, yet when our budgie escaped from his cage one day the cat grabbed him, jumped down from the window with the bird in its mouth and hid under the sideboard. We retrieved the bird after some coaxing and it was completely unhurt, living for years afterwards.

Perhaps Jake enjoyed this immunity. It only made him more swaggery than ever. Like all jackdaws Jake loved shiny objects and in his shed I discovered pieces of silver paper, glass and buttons. If you offered him something shiny he immediately took it in his beak and flew off to examine it at his leisure. He knew my voice from quite a distance away and visitors who didn't know him would often be very surprised to see a big black bird drop out of the skies and land on my head.

"Di ye realise there's a craw sittin on yir heed?"

I pretended that nothing untoward had happened.

"Aye the craws aboot here ir awfy bold, they often dae that."

Jake disgraced himself often. Pud's mother had baked him a birthday cake and left it near the kitchen window to cool. Jake flew in and picked off half the icing before he was discovered. To Pud this was a personal insult, and Pud never forgot a slight. Every incident was stored for future retribution. He was jealous of the jackdaw anyway. His doo was a mean, pitiful bird beside this black, handsome, swaggering crow.

The village children had the best of two worlds, miles of countryside to explore and the amenities of a small town, cinemas, playing fields, cafes and the streets themselves, a concrete playground to which we adapted our games and sports. The girls played paldies. Intricate patterns were drawn on the pavements or streets and a polish tin, filled with mud was moved by the foot, trying to avoid the lines. The girls were very adroit at this, skipping and hopping with bewildering footwork resembling a ritual dance and muttering incantations. They settled their disputes amicably. If boys joined in, there were always arguments over line decisions.

"It wis oan the line." "It wisnae." "It wis so." "Ach, yir a blether, ah'm no playin."

Foot and a half was the boys game, girls completely barred. We started off with a standing jump, toeing a line then leaping forwards as far as possible. Some boys went through an elaborate procedure, bending and stretching their knees rhythmically, arms swinging forwards and backwards, then swinging them violently upwards at the same time bracing the knees and jumping. The boy with the shortest jump was down, legs apart, trunk bent forward from the waist, hands on the thighs. The longest jumper acted as marker. After jumping over the stooping boy's back he stood still and the boy moved to the spot. The rest of the group had then to attempt the jump without touching the base line drawn in chalk. If they all succeeded the marker then took one step before leap-frogging over and the rest followed suit. This could lead to two and over, three and over and so on. The first boy to take more steps than the rest or bowl over the boy in the down position was then the vaulting horse for the next game.

This was a dangerous game on concrete and many cuts and bruises ensued, especially on the head, hands and knees. I'm sure Jackie had a scar for every game of foot and a half. The jumping was great fun but if you were unlucky enough to land as the horse, it was a different matter as, bent forward, hands on the thighs, head tucked down for safety, you gazed at the concrete waiting for that big brute Pud to vault while the young lads sang "All of a sudden, a big mealy pudden, came flying through the air."

Opposite pavements provided many games, the street being the natural hazard in between. 'Walk the plank or join the crew' was another tough game, usually played by boys. One was selected as Pirate Chief in the centre, while the others had to try to get across to the opposite side. Anyone unfortunate enough to be caught was tortured until he got away or agreed to join the crew. The tortures included limbs bent in positions nature never intended, hair rubbed in dung and dirt and similar unpleasantnesses. As the Pirate Chief was usually the biggest and strongest boy, it was policy to join the crew as quickly as possible after a show of bravado then help to catch the others. Craw used to hold out longer than anyone else until I feared for his life.

Like most rough games serious fights started from friendly beginnings. Everything in the street was utilised, the lamp standard a post for 'kick can thirty' and the cross bar a high swing. The iron fences were our tightropes and the big privet hedges trampolines, much to the wrath of their owners. Once, to our amusement, a hedge was damaged by a drunk man. He came staggering up the pavement with his friend, arms swinging wildly to maintain balance, finally collapsing on to the hedge and landing on the flower bed. The other man carried on up the street holding a one sided conversation, unaware that his partner was no longer there. We helped the recumbent drunk to his feet, a rose stuck grotesquely in his hair, and pointed him in the right direction.

Craw found a bottle containing some whisky and, thinking the man had consumed enough, put it in his own pocket. The following day, he soaked some broken bread in the whisky and tossed the scraps into the hen run of a woman who had confiscated his kite. The hens were in an awful state, falling about, cackling foolishly, eyes rolling. Their owner was very puzzled. Was it tick fever or were they egg bound or what?

"You'd think they wir the worse o drink," she confided to a neighbour, "Ah wonder if that Craw and his pals hiv been up tae oanything?"

Boys and girls joined in skipping. The rope was sometimes twelve feet long and two children would caw it while the others skipped in and out in a variety of movements. You were out if you stopped the rope which sometimes coiled fiercely round your neck like a snake or burned like a hangman's noose, depending on the goodwill or otherwise of the cawers. Rounders was an all embracing game. As many as twenty children joined in, aged from five to eighteen. We played at cross roads which formed a natural square to run round with resting stops at each corner. The ball could be hit in four directions away from the gardens though inevitably it bounced too high and landed in one, sometimes to be confiscated.

"Kin a git ma ba back?"

"No ye canny git it back, yir no staunin on ma brussel sprouts."

"Kin wi git it back the moarn thin?"

"Here, tak it for ony favour, noo awa ye go and jump in somebody else's gairden fir a change."

If caught running between corners the fielders had no mercy. They didn't just try to hit you but to bowl you over or knock your head off, so that there was no doubt that you had been hit. A corner was a haven indeed.

We loved it when adults joined in our games. There was often a young-at-heart matron bouncing up and down in the skipping ropes and occasionally a drunk wanting to show his prowess with a rounders bat. The children divided the various householders into two halves. Good and bad or those who gave you your ball back and those who didn't. The latter suffered. In the dark wintry nights, a piece of plasticine with a nail suspended would be stuck on one of their windows with a long length of string stretching from the nail to a hedge or fence. Several of us lay behind the screen and pulling the string in jerks caused the nail to tap repeatedly on the glass.

A face would appear between the curtains, look out suspiciously, much to our mirth, then withdraw until we repeated the performance. Eventually the owner would come outside and start to follow the direction of the string. That was the signal to go. Some of the upstairs houses had doors facing each other. Craw and I occasionally tied the knockers together with a length of clothes rope then rattled the knockers and ran.

This was great fun, the two occupants pulling in a tug of war trying to get out. Very simple laws operated in the street, based on survival at all costs. The strong preyed on the weak.

"Gie's a fag or ah'll batter ye."

The lions had their following of hyenas where cunning was as important as strength. Some boys had to be given deference accordingly. Jackie, Craw and I presenting a solid front were seldom molested. Intelligence or book learning gained little respect.

'Bertie is good at maths,' had no significance. 'Rab Hunter kin dae a handspring, Erchie Watson kin waggle his ears. Sadie Turner hammered Tam Broon. Eckie Hodge pinched wan o his faither's fags, Wee Jim his a swan's egg.' These were the things that impressed us. Some children of course opted out of the gang system or their parents kept them in at night. They were simply classified as swots or snobs and left alone. Occasionally they won cupboard love or respect if they had a new bicycle or football, both very scarce during the war.

"Bertie, ir yi comin oot?" was asked when what was really meant was "Is yir fitbaw comin oot?"

Jake joined in many of the games. He loved to fly after paper aeroplanes and attack them in mid air. At rounders, he flew after the ball and helped us to find it if it landed in long grass. Anything in the air was given his personal attention. It had no right being in his domain without permission. He gave the skipping ropes a wide berth though, after an aerial attack resulted in him being flung violently through the air like a bundle of rags.

FISHING

I followed three paces behind my Father, not allowed any closer.

"Back a bit, back a wee bit more," he whispered urgently. "The fish'll see ye."

It seemed as if we were stalking a tiger rather than small burn trout at Lochornie Burn. We took advantage of every blade of grass and small mound of earth. The larks sang their hearts out in the sky above and the sad mournful call of the whaup made you feel like crying. Lochornie burn was dark peaty brown only a foot wide in places, coming from Loch Glow, a dark dour loch, sulking in bleak moorland and winding its way to join the Black Burn at Keltybridge.

The line tightened suddenly. "Got him," my father shouted delightedly and swung the rod up and round to land a small wriggling fish on the bank. He removed the fly hook expertly. The fish would usually be hooked by the lip only, as father struck very quickly, seeing a flash of white in the water and flicking his wrist simultaneously. If the fish swallowed the hook it was a messy business for man and fish alike, though the fish always came off worst.

Father handed the trout to me. The colours were gorgeous, reds, yellows, browns and blacks, some of the scales coming off in my hands like drops of stardust. I kept the fish alive as long as I could, unwilling to let this vitality fade, by letting it float in small pools cut off from the burn. Father wasn't so sentimental. If the fish was a reasonable size he wouldn't risk me letting it go accidentally, or 'accidentally ma Granny,' as he would say.

A sharp tap over a stone and that was that. Father lit a fire using small dry twigs and grass then took a billy can out of the fishing bag, boiled some water then added tea and sugar. He dropped in a small twig for some reason I've forgotten and boiled it some more. This was the tea of teas, nectar of the hunters. We sat on a wide tree stump and shared the billy can, then father lit a cigarette, scaring the flies away, the smoke merging with that from the fire coiling lazily upwards.

I had the tea to myself now, with a cheese roll Mother had packed. The taste was indefinable, a tang of tin, wood, smoke, fish and carbon. I decided I wanted to be a tramp like Jimmy Peely so I could have tea like this forever.

"Here, there's ants crawlin aboot me," father roared, standing up and brushing down his trousers, breaking my peaceful reverie.

On the larger burns like the Netherton, father fished with what he called the coo dung flea, a large reddish fly. I was the collector. No stalker of exotic butterflies with a net took greater patience than I did with the coo dung fleas, moving forwards one slow step at a time, freezing at the slightest sign of them rising, till I stood close to the cow pies. One quick swipe with a leafy branch and several lay kicking vigorously, too stunned to fly.

I put the undamaged ones in a match box ready for the supreme sacrifice. Father put them on a small bare hook and they were a very effective bait. All fishermen know the thrill of seeing a fly floating lazily on the surface of a gleaming pool, the sudden swirl of water and the bait disappearing as a fish takes. Is it large or small? Some of the small burn trout felt like whales as they struggled fiercely, bending the point of the rod like a bow.

We tried all types of bait. When the water was in spate, the favourite was the black-headed worm, deadly for the 'Lochies' from Loch Leven as they swarmed up the Gairney or the Queich to spawn in October or return in March.

The bramble worm was also popular, a red worm found in the farm dung heaps. Maggots were useful, too, in dark water, though repulsive little things to handle with their white blind squirming bodies. We sometimes put a tin of dead fish behind the shed and waited until the bluebottles laid their eggs and the maggots grew big enough to use. They smelled atrociously but put into a tin of sweet smelling oatmeal they became acceptable company. I remember opening a tin that had been lying in the shed for a week to see if the maggots were still usable. The lid was stiff and it came away suddenly. A swarm of nauseous bluebottles flew right in to my face, buzzing angrily, some getting tangled in my hair, some narrowly missing my mouth and nostrils. I shuddered in fright and distaste and they flew to the window, buzzing even louder, and some tangled in spiders' webs.

To this day I detest these large obscene flies. Strangely enough, maggots could be purchased at the Co-operative chemist's. The manager was a keen fisherman and provided the facility for other enthusiasts on one condition only. Standing at the counter with other customers buying perfume, soap, and other toilet requisites, no one was allowed to ask for 'three dizzen maggots.' The only acceptable term was 'Live bait please…'

My father's favourite bait, however, was the white cob. These were scarce and usually found in the roots of mature dockens where they often burrowed a tunnel right up the centre of the root. Father would dig for hours to obtain a dozen. They weren't as repulsive, somehow, as maggots, as they appeared to have heads and features, while the maggots seemed to have neither. The heads were red and the bodies firm to the touch. He treated them like precious gems, won from the ground and placed them carefully in a cocoa tin filled with soft moss. Many a wary trout was lured from the depths of a pool to the docken cob. The most dangerous bait to obtain was the larvae of wasps. A neighbour informed Jackie and I that there was large wasp byke attached to the underside of his shed roof.

We collected Craw and approached carefully with a box to stand on and a pad soaked in ether scrounged from the District Nurse. Jackie and I climbed slowly on to the box. I held a bag to hold the byke and Jackie had a stick. Craw grinned below as we edged closer to the roof, then suddenly rattled the roof loudly with a garden rake starting an angry drone inside the white dome. We rushed from the shed Craw well in front. Jackie and I returned later without him and this time everything went well. I held the bag open and Jackie knocked the byke down in one swift blow. The wasps inside immediately buzzed angrily and as some stray wasps flew about our heads we moved quickly away from the shed. The buzzing grew faster as the ether took effect and soon all was quiet.

Opening the bag we marvelled at the intricate structure of the byke, paper sculpture at its finest. The wasps were at all stages of development from small white eggs to fully formed black and yellow adults. On the River Eden at Gateside we tried all the different stages of developing wasps. No trout would go near the coloured adults, perhaps the black and yellow acting as a danger signal. The best bait appeared to be those that were fully grown but still white and with those we caught some large trout in the pools. As we had a tin full of larvae left the three of us decided to have a camping and fishing weekend. On the Friday evening we cycled to the Warwicks part of the Queich burn, near Carnbo. Here there was a dark dangerous chasm which opened out into a large deep beautiful pool called The Golden Linn. The small tent was set up quickly and we lit the primus stove and boiled some tomato soup. This was delicious, supping it outside with large chunks of bread.

Craw noticed a carrion crow's nest in a tree overlooking the pool. He climbed quickly and reached the nest built on quite a slender branch. Craw shouted down "There' s only wan in it so ah'll leave it alane."

He had an eye for the dramatic, standing out boldly silhouetted against the sky, the pool far below. He swayed the branches deliberately while we held our breath in suspense. 'Ayeehaa.' his Tarzan call rang through the trees and he swung down, dropping the last six feet on to some soft moss. We sat round the fire and Craw played 'The Rowan Tree' on his chanter.

We murmured the words 'Yir leaves were aye the first o Spring in aw the countryside.'

The darkness came down quickly and a full moon rose, lighting up the Golden Linn like a miniature lake of liquid gold. Small bats fluttered over the tent emitting tiny squeaks as they chased insects.

An owl flapped raggedly close to the ground and little splashing sounds from the Linn indicated trout were rising. Cushy doos murmured sleepily in a nearby wood and we decided it was bedtime for us. Jackie and I woke frozen and shivering an hour later and realised that we didn't have nearly enough blankets with us for the chill of the night. Craw lay sleeping peacefully, his impish face unusually still and cherubic by torchlight. We woke him roughly and demanded turns each in the centre, and so we passed the long still night sleeping one hour out of every three.

Oh the comfort of the centre position, the two outside bodies sheltering the draughts, sheer bliss for an hour. Never did an hour pass so quickly, in no time a rude demanding voice breaking the peace

"C'mon, move over. It's ma turn."

We slept late and woke to a glorious morning, the Golden Linn sparkling in the early sun and the dew cool and caressing on our bare feet. Craw, asserting his leadership again after being ousted from the centre of the tent, suggested that we all dive in simultaneously off an overhanging rock, disdaining the toe, foot, leg, knee, routine favoured by the timid, and not befitting adventurers.

Three boys stood poised on the rock. This was not the Golden Linn of the Queich below but a blue tropical lagoon with pearls as big as doos' eggs. These were not crows in the surrounding trees but macaws and parakeets chattering in excitement.

Ready, steady, Go. Oh the shock of impact then submersion. The linn gripped us in an iron fist, squeezing the heart till it threatened to burst. The pool was fed by hill burns and absolutely freezing. We crawled out immediately, teeth chattering, goose pimpled boys again, no longer noble savages. Craw lit the primus stove and we gathered round warming our hands at the small flame. In no time, he fried some ham and eggs. Unlike mother's they weren't clearly defined but became one object. To us in our hunger, they were delicious.

We walked down the burn, anxious to try the wasps' larvae. To reduce weight on the bikes we had only brought one rod and took turn about fishing, catching several trout, a fine panful for lunch. The rod was heavy and casting difficult. We came to a stretch of the burn where a dilapidated fence separated the narrow bank from a field full of grazing stirks.

We tried not to attract their attention, as irritating flies on a warm day tended to make them erratic and frisky. Jackie swung the rod clumsily, the hook stuck in a wild rose bush and he shook the rod trying to release the barb. The bush bent and rustled attracting the attention of the stirks, and they came charging on us like a troop of cavalry, angrily banging against the flimsy fence. We were very frightened, so, quickly removing our shoes and socks, Craw and I slipped into the burn and waded across, letting out the line of the rod as we did so. Jackie gave up trying to release the hook and struggled with his laces. He broke the second lace in panic and stepped clumsily into the burn, breaking away part of the banking, the wet noses, smoking nostrils and wide eyes of the stirks inches from his face. Incredibly he had disturbed a wild bees' nest in the banking. Some flew at him, buzzing and stinging and he threw his shoes with socks inside at the opposite bank. One landed safely, the other floated away down the burn like a small boat.

We abandoned the rod and fled from the spot, even Craw overawed by the combination of large prancing stirks and small vicious bees. We retrieved Jackie's shoe and sock downstream, the sock still dry. My jacket had become sodden in the excitement so Craw and Jackie offered to dry it for me while I hung on for a while to retrieve the rod. They skirted the field and walked back to the camp then lit a big fire. I waited about a quarter of an hour then approached the rod cautiously.

Several bees were still flying above their ravaged nest, so I cut the line with a pocket knife and left quietly.

"Yir jeckit's dry," Craw shouted at my arrival, "Sorry aboot the burn in it."

A large circular singed area stood out dramatically at the back. At least we had the trout.

"Ma mither wid fry them in oatmeal fir oor tea," I offered tentatively. Craw and Jackie jumped at the chance. None of us fancied another cold night in the tent. We packed quickly and mounted our bikes, whistling like blackies as we left the Golden Linn.

The pike or fresh water shark was a dangerous adversary. There were many of these predators in Lassodie Loch near where my father was born. The loch was ideal for them with shallow water in places where reeds grew in abundance sheltering frogs, young water hens, coots and ducks, all potential food for the pike.

Father promised to take me fishing if I caught some minnows for him, so I went down to the Netherton Burn where minnows were plentiful. At a small pool near Cantsdam a fallen tree formed a bridge across the burn. Sitting on the centre, I threw in a jar filled with bread crumbs attached to a length of string. Soon the minnows appeared, inquisitive but suspicious. They swarmed round and round the jar, wary of the opening but savouring the crumbs, floating out towards them. As a crowd gathered, the boldest or hungriest would dart into the jar. A quick jerk and he was caught, dashing madly round and round his glass prison.

As soon as we had enough, Father and I set off for the loch. As we approached we were astonished to see a plague of frogs. The grass was wet and they seemed to be emerging from a ditch. There were thousands of them, every step we took squashing several bodies, till we started to tiptoe looking for islands in the sea of frogs. Where they were going was not clear, they were hopping in all directions, perhaps like lemmings to sacrifice themselves in some mass suicide attempt.

The pike, I'm sure, would have welcomed them with open jaws. Pike would grab at any bait, even a coloured rag, but seemed to especially like minnows. Father attached a special wire trace with a mount which clipped over the minnow's head and a trailing hook. He flung the line well out clear of the reeds, a cork float bobbing on the surface.

THE DOOKIE

After a few minutes the cork suddenly went under, the great moment when a fisherman knows some fish has taken the bait. A threshing in the water indicated that a fairly large pike was hooked and soon he was pulled to the bank, not really a great fighter for such a fierce fish.

The pike was about two feet long, malevolent eyes and snapping jaws like gin traps. Father stunned it with a stick and placed it in his heavy fishing bag. We fished for an hour with no more takes and as the dark balmy night started to caress us, we walked the three miles home.

The pike seemed dead on arrival, but a faint movement of the gills indicated life. He had been struck on the head with a stick, and out of the water for over an hour. In

India they say a snake never dies until sundown so perhaps pike had their own appointed hour too, maybe midnight. I placed it in the bath, and only the eyes still seemed alive, the slender streamlined body motionless. Like the shark, the pike had a fascinating sinister beauty, the whole body possessing a graceful symmetry designed perfectly for the purpose of catching and devouring the unwary.

Mother called me from my piscatorial perusal to supper, and soon I was fast asleep, tired from the walk home. At two in the morning, I crept to the bathroom, bleary eyed, still half asleep.

I woke with a start. The pike was dashing madly from end to end in the bath, his head cleaving the surface of the water. He slowed down gradually but still his eyes swivelling in my direction balefully. As often happens with humans, fright turned to anger. I drained away the water, threw a thick towel over the pike, took it to the scullery and dispatched it quickly with the blunt end of an axe. In the morning, Mother fried it in batter and we had it for breakfast.

When the boys swam in the Netherton burn they were always aware of the dangers of pike. I do not think there are any recorded instances of pike attacking man but no doubt some people have been injured swimming when the fish has felt trapped in shallow water and found his escape route blocked. Once a boy swimming with us came out of the water with a badly gashed wrist and blamed it on a large fish. The Netherton came from Loch Fitty and some monsters of over three feet have been recorded there.

Father sometimes took me fishing to a burn at Roscobie which eventually ran into Loch Fitty. One fine summer's day the water was low and clear and not very good for fishing. Father was having no luck with the fly so, bored of following him, I started guddling in a pool he had just left. He didn't really approve of this method, being somewhat of a fishing purist.

Standing in a pool with my trousers rolled up as far as they would go, I reached under a big stone merging with the bank. There were several large trout at the furthest point. For some reason, the fish will lie still and allow a guddler to caress its belly. This is known as tickling a trout. I stroked gently, hardly daring to breathe, moving the fish slowly upwards until it pressed against the stone, then pushed one thumb into the gills searching for a grip on the slithery body. I tried to stun it under the water by pressing its head hard against the stone. The trout threshed violently and tried to move further into the banking. I crouched lower in the water and felt my seat wet, one shirt sleeve fell down and floated on the surface. Still the trout moved like a strong spring in my hands. It was now or never. In one movement I pulled it out quickly and flung it on to the bank as it slipped out of my hand anyway. Father arrived saying "It's nae yiss the water's too clear," then catching sight of the trout, added grudgingly, "That's no a bad fish."

I pleaded for one more chance to show him my skills. This time I was too impatient, knowing Father was waiting to go home and, feeling the underbelly of a fish, snatched too quickly. I was horrified to see a young pike about a foot long glide into the pool. A trout darts about in panic but a pike moves more like a submarine with the same deadly air of purpose. This one could have given me quite a bite and put me off guddling for a while afterwards.

Trout too can turn cannibal and adopt the characteristics of the pike. The Black Burn sometimes dried up in the summer, leaving only shallow pools where trout splashed anxiously about. Several years ago some miners feeling sorry for the fish, gathered a bucket of them and placed them in an old small disused quarry filled with water. Craw and I heard that they had turned cannibal and the survivors were enormous. We walked several miles into Blairadam forest and reaching the pool, crept on our hands and knees and peered into the gloomy depths.

Great slabs of rock lay piled up forming dark sinister valleys where no bottom could be seen. Occasionally shafts of sunlight struck the rock like a searchlight. All at once a long shape moved into our vision. The trout was about the length of a forearm, exactly as described, with a slim body and large head. It swam with the look of a predator, slowly, missing nothing. No frogs croaked in the shallows of the pool.

A light drizzle of rain started but we tried a line baited with worms for several minutes with no success and decided to leave. The general gloom of the quarry surrounded by dark, dripping spruce trees appeared to have hidden secrets that we felt no inclination to solve.

THE SUNDAY SCHOOL

We had very few rules in our house and enjoyed a lot of freedom, but one thing was insisted on. We had to go to Sunday School until we were fourteen, then decide whether to continue or not. Mother was in the Brethren, who met in the Gospel Hall, a small red corrugated iron building down Station Road. This was a snug, warm place in the winter. Children of all ages sat round a large black iron stove in the centre, with a long pipe disappearing through the roof. The stove would get very hot and when the preacher wasn't looking we would sometimes spit on it, watching the tiny balls of moisture roll, hiss and disappear into a puff of steam.

This was much better than the cold, austere atmosphere of the Church. The Hall emitted such a warm friendly atmosphere that backward adults, children who had never grown up, would join us, knowing that they would be accepted and welcomed. No one was allowed to tease these unfortunates. The preachers were grand men, sure in their faith, strict when necessary, humorous and humble. They delivered strong, sometimes frightening sermons. Heaven and Hell became real places, not something to hide away in the mind for future reference. There seemed few grey areas, black or white, good or evil, and the Devil was a force to be reckoned with, lurking always in shadowy places, waiting to catch the unwary.

It seemed he was especially fond of Kelty Cross, where pubs stood on two corners with a bookie's shop only slightly further up the road. Even to loiter there was dangerous. Perhaps this was why Uncle Tommy chose it as his battleground. What courage! He was a miner working underground with many tough and, coarse men. At the weekends he stood alone at The Cross, playing a small portable harmonium and preaching the gospel.

I remember him vaguely as a small stout cheery man always with a poke of sweets for the children. Some of my father's friends asked him if his brother-in-law wasn't a bit odd.

"No, he's the wisest man in the village," he told them.

We sat on long brown varnished seats in the Sunday School, singing all the old redemption hymns from little red books, and sometimes from a large sheet the preacher hung from the wall. Great songs, vibrating round the Hall, filling or throats and hearts, making the tin roof rattle in chorus.

We knew the ten commandments by heart. Most of them seemed to apply to grown ups but one stood out to us - 'Thou shalt not steal.' Mother applied the rule rigidly. Any money found had to be taken to the Police Station, and no strawberries or pears were to be stolen from other gardens.

I found a hen under a hedge sitting on one egg and took it home, persuading my elder sister to boil it for my tea, as Mother was going to be late. She discovered me at my stolen meal. The next morning I was sent back with another egg. The Hen Man must have been very puzzled to find an egg under his hen with a stamp on it.

At Christmas time the Hall filled to capacity for a soirée. We were served with hot sweet tea, pies and cakes. Everyone had to perform a poem or song in front of parents. The hero of a poem, 'The Covenanter's Boy' bore the same name as myself. When the Preacher came across it he said "Oh, there's only one person for this."

I loved the poem actually. There were some really dramatic pieces in it and I performed these with gusto.

"I'll throw you o'er the mountainside and there among the stanes,

The old gaunt wolf and carrion crow will battle for your banes."

Everyone's favourite, however, was the 'Ten Little Candles.' Ten of the smallest children stood on the small stage, each holding a lighted candle. The hall lights were put out and all eyes focussed on the stage. Each child said a short piece then blew out a candle, starting from one end, the tallest down to the smallest child. Some were confident, speaking loud and clearly, others rushing through as quickly as possible.

One or two of the really wee ones required whispered prompting. The last child lit her neighbour's candle again and so on until all the candles glowed as before to tremendous applause.

Many adults in the village must recall taking part in Ten Little Candles, the one time you were allowed to play with fire with permission.

THE DUMP

The dump was a magnet for magpie boys. We spoke of going for a rake in the dump like going to the pictures. It was amazing what people threw out. We raked with our boots, uncovering untold treasures. Tools, toys, ornaments, photographs, old roller skates and bikes. I would stagger home with the booty, a vase for Mother, a screwdriver and nails for Father. They stopped me going for a while after I took home a long box full of interesting tubes and funnels.

"Tak that back right away," Father roared, "that's fir washin oot the bowels."

This conjured up all sorts of images like the bowels hanging up on a clothes line to dry, but, back it had to go. As Jackie and I raked, we unearthed a cardboard box. To our amazement the lid started to rise. "Rats," Jackie whispered and grabbed a stick. He prized the lid off and discovered three kittens, not long born, mewing pitifully, feebly struggling. Someone had just dumped them in a rubbish bin. We took them back, found homes for them and all three grew into handsome cats.

The dump was situated in an old quarry with an abandoned mine shaft, attracting many children and occasional adults. There was always at least one scruffy man, with a wooden barrow made out of a box and pram wheels, poking away in the ashes. We made fire-cans out of syrup tins punched with holes. These were filled with little bits of paper, sticks and coal. Holding a long wire, we burled them round and round our heads to stoke the flames. Inevitably we set fire to the dump, resting a can on top of an old mattress. Jackie and Craw tried to stamp it out while I rushed with a can to a stagnant pool of water. It was too late, the dump was on fire. Auld Downie, the supervisor, whose house overlooked the quarry, came running over, threatening Police, Borstal and other dire punishments. I think the dump smouldered for a week before dying out. It was fairly safe really, well away from any houses.

We lay behind rocks when the horse and cart arrived, like Indians ambushing a waggon train and as soon as it departed, we whooped down, trying to be first to reach the treasures.

The dump attracted flocks of birds, mostly gulls, crows and starlings. The three of us set up primitive traps for the starlings, three bricks forming an enclosure with a fourth in the centre propped up by a stick. The trap was baited with scraps of food and as soon as a starling went in, the string pulled. It was a surprisingly effective trap though birds could be easily injured. An old riddle was better if one could be found.

Rats were everywhere in the dump. Food was plentiful and supported a large colony. Always when we arrived a few could be seen disappearing into their runs. They were our sworn enemies and we spent many hours trying to trap them. We had an impressive array of traps. One trap was like a giant mousetrap, another the dreaded gin-trap and we also had cages.

Some nights we would wait for hours listening for the click, then run over to see what manner of beast we had caught. Once, a weasel lay in the gin trap. The rats were usually killed outright by the neck, but occasionally one would be held in a gin trap by a paw or even a tail. They looked very vicious, chattering and showing their teeth. These were dispatched with sticks. The man at the stables caught them in cages and dumped them into a barrel of water. The rats sought desperately for freedom swimming round and round the cage, testing every possible escape, biting at the wires, taking a long time to drown.

We caught one in a cage and took it to a field near the dump, to give it a sporting chance. Lucky, our dog, was with us and gave chase as soon as the door was opened. He caught the rat then dropped it, caught it again and let it go. By this time the rat was wet and bedraggled with saliva.

Lucky, a mongrel must have had a gun dog in his ancestry. He refused to kill the rat and it eventually escaped down a hole. Lucky loved digging for rats, spending hours in a hole with earth and ashes flying cut like bullets. He never caught a rat this way but sometimes unearthed a nest. The young ones were usually bare and blind, so helpless looking it was difficult to dislike them. We saw the Head Forester in the field next to the dump with a cage and went over to see what was going on. A grey squirrel was in the cage and bore no resemblance to his kind in Pittencrieff Park. It gnawed constantly at the cage showing sharp ferocious teeth. The Forester put a thick wire through the spars and the squirrel immediately grabbed it and left a large dent. We shuddered at this display of biting. The Forester had a young fox terrier he wanted to train to hunt. He prodded the squirrel again to make it scamper round the cage, the dog getting more and more excited. The cage was opened and the squirrel made a dash for the woods, fifty yards away. The dog caught it easily and the squirrel sank its teeth into the terrier's nose making the dog yelp in anguish. He dropped the squirrel and it ran again. This time the dog made no mistake. He killed the squirrel quickly and worried the carcase. Amazingly, what had seemed a pup changed, in a few seconds, into a dog, the hairs of the neck standing out, jaws snapping and eyes as black as coal. No rat would bite him again, I thought. We once tried to kill rats with homemade bows and arrows tipped with two inch wire nails tied on with wire.

After several unsuccessful attempts Craw said, "Pile up some tin cans, Jackie, and we'll try to knock them down."

Jackie, ever obliging, started to do this while Craw and I drew our bows in readiness. Craw's arrow slipped and the nail stuck into Jackie's arm making him howl with pain. Craw, the leader, was embarrassed at his mistake and apologised but, seeing that the wound wasn't deep, said, "I'm sorry, I mistook ye fir a rat." Jackie produced the box of sticking plaster his mother made him carry. He grew quite proud afterwards.

"No many boys hiv been shot wi an arrow nooadays," he said.

A road with telegraph poles passed the dump and ritually we tied the rats to a string and threw them up into the air until they tangled in the wire, our own unique gibbet, and some of the carcases remained there for months to be picked at by crows and gulls. Auld Downie encouraged us to catch rats.

"Kill as many as ye can. They carry disease and, if ye can catch a hundred, ah'll no tell the polis ye set fire tae the dump."

Kelty Silver Bell Cycling Club

THE BOYS CLUB

Mondays and Thursdays were Boys Club Nights held in Oakfield School Gymnasium. The school itself was gradually subsiding due to underground workings, and a six inch incline was not uncommon in some rooms. Through the years, as the doors jammed, joiners had cut pieces off the bottom rails to fit the floor and the shape of the rails gave some indication of the obvious cant. There were cracks all over the building and the school gave the appearance of being ready to subside at any moment. The gym, however, was a more recent building and the floor was level.

The Fife Miners Boys Clubs were a big asset to communities. Practically every village had a club and a district organiser came round regularly, passing on information on courses, boxing championships, football and athletic contests. The leaders were voluntary and many men gave up their leisure time to instruct the boys in all the club activities. The Kelty Silver Bell Cycling Club had recently disbanded and several of the members who were very fit and energetic came to help in the Boys Club, so that we had instructors in the different sections. As today, adult interest sparked off great enthusiasm among the children. The boys themselves were generally quite a tough bunch. PT kit was their dress or even just a vest, long trousers and stocking soles, as sandshoes were considered a luxury in some families. Few of them attended uniformed organisations such as the cubs or scouts. There was no tying knots or kids games for them. The games had to be like themselves, tough and demanding.

In a game called Commandos, two teams were chosen and a mat placed at either end of the gym. The purpose was to pull the other side on to your own mat, where they had to remain until the end of the game. It was like a free-for-all fight. The smaller boys were grabbed first of all and dumped unceremoniously on a mat to cut down numbers a bit. The bigger boys then tried to isolate a victim from his team mates and pull him by sheer weight of numbers. Boys would be hauled by the feet, their backs sliding along the floor, picking up splinters and friction burns, sometimes to be flung from a height like a sack of potatoes on to an already overcrowded mat.

Pirates was the most dangerous game, banned at day schools. All the apparatus was put out for this, vaulting boxes, mats, beams, ropes and benches. A pirate chief would be chosen by the leader and he had to catch the rest. The apparatus represented a galleon with rigging, and the empty spaces on the floor, the sea. A boy was out when the chief touched him or he landed in the sea.

Oakfield gym was small and ideally suited to the game. It was possible to swing from one set of beams to the other on the ropes and from one vaulting box to another. Just imagine, thirty boys jumping, swinging, running up benches fixed to the top wall bars, walking precariously along beams several feet off the ground, jumping through the air to catch ropes , and sliding down them or swinging to a piece of apparatus. We helped each other, swinging a rope to a trapped friend, pulling up someone hanging from the end of a vaulting box, his feet inches off the floor.

The game was so popular no one wanted to be out and leaders were constantly bawling the paradoxical, "C'mon, get aff - yir oot."

There were many minor accidents of course, cuts, bruises, sprains, none fatal in my time. Boxing was made more or less compulsory, part of the toughening up process. The ring was formed with four PE benches. Two minutes seem a very short time but we boxed three two minute rounds and it seemed like an eternity. I still recall the smell of leather and sweat, the taste of warm blood in the mouth, eyes watering after receiving a punch full on the nose, trying to smile in case anyone thought you were crying.

Boxing with Craw and Jackie presented problems, but personal honour was at stake and we tore into each other as hard as if we were fighting our worst enemies. The leaders usually matched the boys in size or weight but, occasionally, you landed with a bruiser a stone heavier or much taller than yourself. It was a case then of counter-punching on the retreat, relying on nimble footwork to get out of trouble or hoping the leader would intervene to stop further punishment.

The club operated a natural selection process The weak, the nervous and perhaps the wise came one night and didn't return, perhaps joining the cubs or scouts promising to do their best and their duty to God and The King, not promising to fight three rounds with some ruffian intent on half killing them. Inevitably the rough games and the boxing left some unfinished scores to be settled. On the way home the leaders were surrounded by small groups of boys requiring protection.

There were two ways of achieving status at the club, being good at boxing or vaulting, which at the top level required considerable courage, with headsprings, handsprings and long vaults but the real test was the somersault. In this you ran, bounced on the springboard, turned a complete somersault in the air above a high box and landed on your feet if you were lucky. The mats for landing on were not very thick and you could receive quite a jolt. The somersaulters joined the elite of the club.

At first, four strong boys would hold a mat high and they caught you no matter how you fell but it was quite a step from there to trying it on your own. Another spectacular vault was The Flying Angel. In this the vaulter took a high bounce and flew through the air, arms stretched sideways to be caught by the leader who kept shouting 'Higher, Higher' until some of the high flyers were in danger of going straight over his head to an unknown destination.

Kelty Boys Club was a great training kitchen in strength, agility, courage and toughness, if you could stand the heat. Shortly after Jackie, Craw and I joined, many of the leaders from the old Silver Bell Club married and with added responsibilities were unable to attend so often and eventually stopped coming altogether. The club was without a leader for a while until the organiser made enquiries in the village.

A new leader arrived, freshly demobbed from the army. Joe Steele was tough, no doubt about that. He had been a sergeant in the Army Physical Training Corps and knew his business. He was a good boxer, footballer and a first class sprinter, competing at the Highland Games. Joe applied army discipline to the club and the boys responded well. As soon as he blew his whistle everyone had to stand still and listen to his instructions. Anyone not complying quickly enough was given twelve press-ups at double time. The organisers, on a visit, mentioned that bad language seemed prevalent among many of the boys. After he left Joe decided to give us a pep talk.

"If I hear any more b.........swearing tonight you'll all be sent home b........ well early."

We got the message just the same and, after a few swearings from Joe, the language improved slightly or went under cover. Joe joined in all the games himself. He played Pirates, boxed the bigger boys hitting them just hard enough to let them see who was the master, and vaulted better than any of us. Pud was nearly his Nemesis. A game of basket ball was in progress, spectators sitting on the top wall bars and as usual Joe was refereeing but also playing for the weaker side. Craw passed him the ball and he jumped high to place the ball in the net.

Unfortunately Pud jumped late to defend and as Joe came down his nose met Pud's big baw heid coming up. Joe was in a terrible state, his nose was broken, starting to swell visibly and dripping blood like water from a tap. The boys were very good, helpful and solicitous. One ran for the janitor, another for a cold sponge from the sink. Good leaders were scarce, they had to be encouraged to stay on. Pud was loudly railed for his carelessness. Joe was back as usual the following week. It wasn't really retaliation on Joe's part a fortnight later. Pud deserved what was coming to him. He loved the Boys Club, never managed the somersault, but excelled at games requiring pushing, pulling, tugging and wrestling, where his strength, cunning and weight were an advantage. He enjoyed boxing, too, providing he was matched with a younger, frailer opponent.

On the nights he was matched properly he had a repertoire of excuses, sprained wrist, sore head or hand, staved big toe. Pud was full of tricks. During the compulsory warming up period of exercises, boys would hang from the beams, ready for pull ups. Pud would select a victim, then quickly pull down the boy's shorts to his ankles causing a roar of laughter at the unfortunate who always hung for a few moments, stunned into immobility.

Joe noticed this once or twice then arranged for four of the bigger boys to act at the next pant pulling prank. Pud's laughter changed to consternation, as they grabbed him, took hold of a limb each and rushed him to the big sink at the end wall of the gym. There they pulled down his shorts and turned on the tap. Unfortunately one turned on the hot tap instead of the cold, and Pud was scalded. Though not severely burned, the indignity and embarrassment ended his pull downs at the pull ups.

Soon Joe had an assistant, big Bertie Black, who taught us weight training. He was a well built man and astonished us with feats of muscle control. Bert could suck in his stomach and then press out the centre part only, something he called mid isolation. He could also make many of his muscles dance to the mouth organ and, for the first time, we heard of lats, biceps, triceps and quadriceps.

"Look," Craw whispered in awe, "He's even goat muscles oan his muscles."

He taught us several of the tricks and we discovered that, by pressing the hands hard together in front of the face, the chest muscles or pecks as Bert called them jumped out, and by trying to bend an elbow against resistance from the opposite hand the bicep muscles stood out

"Like a knot in a thread," Pud said scornfully to Jackie's attempt.

Bert was so used to practising muscle control that on passing a mirror he automatically raised his chest and sucked in his stomach to study his reflection for a brief moment. Joe didn't believe in weight training but favoured Swedish drill, a system of free exercises. Watching Bert heaving weights about, he muttered darkly. "He'll git muscle bund."

Father's canaries got egg bund, a door in the house was hinge bund, and now our hero Bert was to be muscle bund. No one seemed to know exactly what the terms meant.

Joe Steel ran a small professional school of runners, including Bert, in the village and was always on the look out for new talent. He soon noticed that Craw, Jackie and I excelled in the relay races in the Gym and invited us to train with him as junior members of the school.

Subconsciously, we had been preparing ourselves for years for competitive running. Before coming in contact with Joe we ran and ran for the sheer joy of it. It was to us as natural as breathing and like breathing, required no conscious thought. Our limbs moved like well oiled hinges, easily, effortlessly. We ran from furious farmers, galloping gardeners, grunting gamekeepers, leering lechers and lascivious landlords. We ran from buzzing bees, skeery stirks, vicious wasps and belligerent bulls. We ran, not on carefully mowed green running tracks but on hard, tough terrain and, as we ran the blood flowed to our legs and away from our heads till we felt light-headed, and floated like thistledown blown by the wind. We were weightless then, hedges and fences no longer obstacle but slight undulations on the course, up and over, on and on, three boys on one black stallion, wild, free, unfettered, whinnying to the wind in an ecstatic surge of life force. We ran for fun, for freedom, from real or imagined dangers, for youth, zest, the joy of living, to be first to reach the morning sun, the hazy rainbow and the evening star; kindred of the fox outstripping the hounds, the hare outrunning the whippet. We ran because we had to. It was quicker than walking, an integral part of nature, the weapon of the hunter, the natural defence of the hunted.

We chased rabbits we had no chance of catching, but enjoying the privilege of entering a race against such runners. We ran first of all for the love of it, then for honour and eventually, more mundanely, for money. In Joe's school we were classified, not just runners but sprinters, middle distance, and marathon runners. I was a sprinter, Jackie specialised in the half mile and Craw trained for the boys' marathon, two miles. We helped each other as pacemakers. In the marathon Jackie and I ran several laps each with Craw, and they both helped me in the sprints, in staggered starts, Jackie benefiting in both types of races and, occasionally, given a chance of his own distance.

Craw wasn't too fast but had great stamina and seemed able and willing to run all day. Playing the chanter at pipe band practice exercised his lungs and controlled his breathing. Our lives were to be restricted from now on, Joe told us, no cycling, swimming, skating, or anything that used the wrong muscles. There was to be no smoking, late nights or excessive eating. The calf muscles became very important, more so than the others. They had to be kept loose, rubbed with liniment, massaged, pampered. The calves were the source of power, the prime points of propulsion. We inspected them regularly, anxiously tapping with the fingers, and they had to quiver like a jelly, no tightness, no strain.

Sandshoes were now inadequate and despised. Father spent some of his hard earned money on my first pair of spiked shoes. With the sandshoes went black gym shorts and cotton vests. Now we wore silk vests and running shorts with stripes and V shaped slits at the sides. The metamorphosis was complete.

"Silk purses out of sow's ears," Joe said proudly.

We competed in inter Boys Club sports and won most of our races. The other boys had only run against humans, never with the rabbit or the hare. Before every race, we stood like fledglings with open mouths and Joe put a spoonful of glucose into our mouths for instant energy. He timed us on a stop watch to fractions of a second and made us aware of the magical even time, one hundred yards in ten seconds, ten yards in a second. Of the few in Scotland who could do it, Joe was one of them. These elite became our heroes unlike the footballers of most boys. Gordon Smith of Hibs meant little to me. I admired Walter Spence of Blyth, back marker at Powderhall and the fastest professional sprinter in Britain.

We were members of a school, with rival schools lurking in the background, ready to steal our training methods and times. Joe altered the standard races if he thought anyone was spying on us so that we ran one hundred and ten yards, and two hundred and thirty yards, to throw them off the scent. I had a mental picture of a man in a dark coat with a black beard lying behind tree stump, stop watch in hand.

Joe took his runners to remote inaccessible places, sometimes away from prying eyes, like Windyedge, a field near an abandoned mine where the wind and rain usually won; and to disused railway tracks with small draughty tin sheds where we changed into running gear like beasts of the field, sheltering from the elements. We trained in the heat of summer and the cold of winter and were greeted in the village now, not by our names, but "How's the runner?" and told "You're being trained by a professional now," as if we were performing animals, as in a way we were.

There was one other school in the village run by Alf Arnott. He and Joe were bitter rivals and this spread to the respective boys in their charge. Neep was a nephew of Alf's and now trained with him. He was a natural runner, long, loose-limbed and single minded. He took after his mother. She ran off with a soldier and left him with his father who brought the boy up on his own.Eck Napier was a dour man and, when his wife left him, he became morose and withdrawn. He had never achieved much in his life and tried to realise his hopes in his son. Neep was a good scholar and his father kept him in every night for at least an hour to do homework, treating his son much the same as his two whippets. He fed them well, exercised them constantly, and didn't believe in too much show of affection or softness. His wife had proved that softness didn't pay. He had handed over his wages every Friday in exchange for cigarettes and the price of a pint and where was she now?

The few times Neep and I had run against each other, the honours had been shared fairly equally, but the Gala Day would be the time of reckoning. In front of the whole village, we would have to pit our speed and stamina against each other. The two trainers added to the tension. Their reputations were at stake when their proteges clashed in competition.

As the rivalry grew, Neep and I passed each other in the street with brief sidelong glances like two dogs sizing each other up. When the Gala Day arrived, Neep was going to be the one to beat.

Alf Arnett's school, too, sought out lonely parts of the countryside to train and sometimes unintentionally the two schools met. Joe and Alf thought this was deliberate and both muttered threats until one moved off the chosen field. No-one wanted to tangle with Joe Steele, though. He was an imposing figure, six foot two, strong shoulders, tapered chest and muscular legs. He kept a close-cropped army-style haircut, had a tanned face with blue eyes, even teeth and a slightly hooked nose. He still wore the crossed sword badge of the Physical Training Corps and this added to his mystique.

"Ye nivver ken whit thae army boys kin dae," my father remarked mysteriously.

Joe and Alf seemed to detest each other more than their rivalry warranted. No one quite knew why, but it went back to their youth and neither man would offer an explanation.

At training Joe was strict and kept us under a tight rein. Craw and Bertie Black provided most of the laughs. Bertie was great fun. He was a good all rounder without excelling in any one event. He could sprint, run a mile, jump, hop step and leap, trying to make up in versatility what he lacked in specialisation. He was a tall handsome chap, liked by men and admired by women though, so far, no girl had lured him into matrimony. Perhaps none came up to his high standards. On the surface Bert had everything going for him, but he couldn't help boasting slightly. If any of the other athletes mentioned an achievement, Bert could always go one better. As they say in Fife, all his eggs were double yoked. At thirty years old, he had done everything, been in the army, the pits, worked in Canada and was now at Rosyth Naval Base. Joe counted up the years that Bert said he had spent in each job and it came to fifty.

Bert was great at cheering us up on a grey early morning training session, was never malicious, and always able to laugh at himself. He was quite an inspiration to the younger runners as we did press ups on the grass, up down, up down, hoping to build muscles like his. With his vanity and tall stories, Bert was a natural target for pranksters. He was an excellent dancer and often went to the Palais at Cowdenbeath. The old-time dances were demonstrated by a Kelty man who had lost a leg in an accident and used a crutch. This didn't seem to affect his dancing ability and he and his partner performed all the intricate steps necessary. As soon as a new dance was demonstrated, Bert grabbed a partner and usually managed to be the first on the floor, dazzling the crowd with his virtuosity.

One night, a group of Kelty dancers were walking home past Kirk o Beath cemetery. It was a dark windy night and Bert, after seeing a girl home, hurried to catch up. Two men dodged into the cemetery, and climbed up on to the high stone wall. Bert couldn't see the crowd, hearing only the faint sound of voices ahead and he increased his pace. Suddenly an unseen force lifted his bonnet from his head and he knew it was not the wind. At the Highland Games he must have held at least one record, the most wins at the Consolation Race. His years of training came into play and he did a hundred yards in what was probably his fastest time ever.

There were no Amateur Athletics Clubs in Fife at the time, and after school athletics, athletes had the chance of running professional or not at all. Edinburgh and Glasgow were too far away to travel or pay the fare for most boys. There were usually about twelve or so runners in Joe's school, six men and six boys. Some stayed with him for years, others left after disagreements on training methods, or perhaps were lured to other schools with the promise of a better handicap at the games. In the same way, we were joined by other runners from time to time. They came from all walks of life. At one time we had an engineer, a mechanic, a bus driver, a miner and a carpenter, a fine bunch of men, all fitness fanatics and seldom crude with the younger boys. Few drank or smoked.

Occasionally we ran against the older men if they required pacemakers but mostly stayed in our own group. As with the men, Joe gave us handicaps at training. I was the fastest sprinter among the junior section and in the short races was usually the back marker or as it was sometimes called offscratch. The other boys had various starts according to their ability. In the half mile, Jackie was the back marker and Craw in the marathon. Handicaps were increased or decreased according to progress. Joe recorded times and handicaps in a little black book which we were never allowed to scrutinise.

In the sprints we spent ages practising starts. Joe kept a little hammer for punching holes in hard ground and the distance between the front and back foot had to be exact.

Starting drill was always the same. We stood five yards back from the holes. "Get to your marks," Joe cried.

Forward, foot dug carefully into the hole, then with a flourish, the back one. Hands forward, foot and opposite knee in the same line. "Get set." Up on the fingertips, leaning forward to the point of balance, back leg braced.

The sudden crack of the pistol seemed to galvanise your whole body into whip like action, arms brought up quickly, fingers spread, slicing the air like scimitars and the race was on. Theories were given to us about the best way to run one hundred yards. "Do it in one breath," or "Run the first twenty five yards full out, cruise the middle fifty, and save something for the last twenty five".

As soon as the race started, we tended to forget all about theories, took as many breaths as required and ran full out all the way. At that time, before the mile became so popular, the one hundred yards sprint was THE race.

At the most important professional meeting of the year, the Powderhall New Year Handicap in Edinburgh, the first prize was a hundred and fifty pounds and a gold medal. In comparison, the mile and half mile were worth fifty pounds each. Sprinters were the aristocrats of the games, the thoroughbreds of running and, like racehorses, tended to be edgy and temperamental. A gun shot from a nearby wood made a sprinter jump instinctively. The bursting of a balloon made the calf muscles tense and ready, responding to conditioned reflexes.

Joe put a great emphasis on style. He had a smooth, effortless action himself. No speed should be lost by a nodding head and flapping arms. He despaired of my gait, right shoulder drooping.

"You're like the leaning tower of Pisa," he sighed "Ah'll hae ti straightin ye up."

"There's a man in our street had a whippet that leaned tae wan side," Craw offered, "an he put some lead in the opposite ear."

"Hoo did he dae that?" I asked. "Wi a shotgun," laughed Craw.

Joe lifted up a brick. "Here, hud this in yir left hand and dae three laps o the track and we'll see if that helps."

So every time I trained Joe made me use the brick for several of the laps. Years later I discovered that this would accentuate the lean rather than help. Joe eventually decided that the brick was no use and I took great pleasure in throwing it into the Black Burn. "You are an unorthodox runner," he said. This sounded a grand title and made up for my disappointment at lack of style.

Several girls started training with Joe and this made the boys run faster than ever trying to impress them. I admired a quiet girl, Mary McIntosh. She ran as effortlessly and gracefully as a roe deer, long fair hair flowing behind her. She occupied my dreams at nights, always running while I followed clumsily, never able to catch up. She was a worthy successor to Rosita.

Sometimes I took Jake with me to training and all the runners made a fuss of him.

"He's aye combin his hair, jist like Bert," one of the men said.

"Is this yir brither, then, Craw?" asked another.

Jake never quite got used to the gun. The first time it went off near him, he took off and flew fifty yards away. After that I steadied him by a leg as he rose in the air two feet in alarm.

"Let's see how fast he can go." Joe said.

The three of us walked down to the fifty yard mark and Joe shouted "Try to beat him over the hundred."

He held Jake protesting on his arm.

We raced to the flag with Jake in hot pursuit and I called his name as I ran. He caught up with us just before the finish and I felt for a moment the primitive fear of being attacked from the air, as a hare feels the draught of an eagle's wings, when Jake gripped my bare shoulder leaving deep scratches.

"Aye, he'll make a sprinter aw richt." Joe roared in delight.

Jake was always attracted to the training bags, picking away at the spiked shoes, harness, extra laces and the coloured flags. Rummaging in Bert's open bag he upset a tin of talcum powder and, as the irate owner ran up, quickly snatched a protector pouch with straps and flew to a nearby tree.

"Git that back or ah'll thraw its neck," Bert said to me in pretended fury.

"Whit dae ye call that funny looking thing, anyway?" I whispered to Craw

"A joke strap," he murmured knowledgeably.

One cold morning we changed into our running gear in a field next to the Black Burn. Benarty's brow was starting to emerge from the mist and the day promised warmth later. The burn gurgled its way to the Meedies, dark and sad as always. There were lots of cows in the field and they gazed at us with mild reproachful eyes.

"Auld Watson's bannet blew off his heid when he walked his whippet here last nicht," Craw said, joking as always. "He tried oan three in the dark before he fund the richt wan."

We shuddered in mock distaste.

"C'mon lads, Cut oot the cackle," Joe roared, "Yi're runnin time trials today."

We lined up. I was scratch in the centre, Jackie off five yards to my right, and Craw off ten yards to my left. The gun spoke and we sprang from our marks, glad to be moving in the cold air. As Jackie and Craw ran, they veered inwards, gradually forming a wedge. At the fifty yard mark we were neck and neck and suddenly, sandwiched by the other two, I tripped and fell headlong into an enormous cow's pie, like a diver, belly flopping into the swimming pool. It was like being in the grasp of a giant jellyfish.

I was covered all over with the thick brown nauseous excrement, in the hair, eyes and mouth, up the nose and ears, squeezed in as if by an outsize toothpaste tube. I had laughed when Craw fell with the rotten egg in his mouth and now it was his turn. He and Jackie lay quivering in the grass, helpless with laughter. Craw tried to get up and fell down again in another frenzy. I stood up, blowing like a whale, opening and closing my eyes in an effort to see.

"Yiv pit yir fit in it this time," Craw moaned weakly, trying in vain to rise.

The Black Burn was bitterly cold. Joe and Bert Black standing barefoot in the water, scrubbed me down until I emerged as pink and shiny as a baby. The taste remained with me for days afterwards, my hearing impaired and eyes dark rimmed. Was it worth all the effort? A snatch from Lycidas crept into my thoughts "Fame is the spur that the clear spirit doth raise, to scorn delights and live laborious days."

We certainly lived laborious days. Up at seven on Sunday mornings, some nights running till dusk, limbs aching in the morning. But the Gala Day and the magical title 'Champion'was getting nearer. To be the best, that's what it was all about.

Football team with some Boys Club members

THE KILLING

Jake was becoming a problem, I thought. He was spending much more time with the jackdaws at the chimney pots and in the trees overlooking the Black Burn. Once or twice I called him and he answered but never came. I was forced to leave him out several times at night and was very worried in case anything happened to him but, the following morning, there he was at the scullery window, tapping at the glass with his beak wanting in for breakfast. He made all sorts of peculiar noises as if he was trying to speak.

"Slit his tongue wi a silver sixpence and he'll talk," an old miner told me.

I declined his advice fortunately for Jake. It reminded me of the old joke about the nephew with a bad stammer visiting his aunt who had acquired a large parrot. "Ca, ca, can, i, i, it, t, t, talk?" he asked.

"Aye, better than you," said the parrot angrily.

I wanted to hold on to Jake for at least another summer. Then, I promised myself, I would take him back to the Cleish Crags, where he was born, well away from humans who would wish him harm. He was as affectionate as ever. When I took him to the shed at night he wanted to roost on my arm, not his perch. He would crouch down, ruffle his feathers to take in a cushion of air, close his eyes and go to sleep, complete trust in human beings. He protested at being wakened but after several attempts, hopped on to his perch, croaked a good night, then resumed his sleep. He had been with me now for two years, as fine a pet as any boy could wish for.

Tame jackdaws inevitably came to a tragic end, their trust betrayed. One or two boys had thrown stones at him and Jake was straying more and more into gardens near Braewell, picking at flowers and vegetables. If Henry caught him, I was afraid that Jake would disappear without trace. Pud had never forgiven him for stealing the icing off his birthday cake and chased him off whenever Jake tried to make friendly overtures to his doo.

A mother had complained to me that Jake had landed on her pram and tried to snatch the baby's rattle. I looked at the bold black crow on my wrist.

Jake, Jake - rogue, thief, vagabond, persecutor of the grey cat, tooth picker, friend, companion. I took you from the wild and to the wild you shall return, to join the great family of jackdaws calling and soaring, quarrelling and loving over the steep crags of Cleish. But not yet, not yet, blue-eyed Jake, not till the end of summer.

I still locked him in the shed when I was at school so that he wouldn't get into difficulties when I was unable to help, but Jake was finding the shed too confining after tasting so much freedom in the evenings and at the week-ends. He started cawing incessantly for long periods and flapping at the shed window like a moth trying to escape. Mother wanted to let him out but I said it was too dangerous when I was away. One day I arrived home from school to find the shed door open and no sign of Jake. I had been doing some running training so was an hour later than usual.

"Who let the bird oot?" I angrily asked Mother.

"It was me," she said defensively, "he's been makin an awfy racket the day and I couldn't stand it any longer."

I went into the garden again and called him. As always, the wild jackdaws made a clamour, some recognising my voice now, but no distinctive answering call among them. No Jake came flying from the trees to greet me with delight. He had always answered before even though he didn't always come right away now. I walked in the field bordering the back gardens calling his name constantly. A neighbour had seen him in the afternoon

"He was sittin oan Pud's doo crib," " she told me.

It started to get dark and I became very worried. I hated Jake to be out all night, he was far safer in the shed. Wandering disconsolately into the house, I complained bitterly to mother.

 "Ah telt ye nivver tae let him oot durin the day."

"He'll turn up, he always does," she said unsympathetically, washing a huge pile of dishes in the sink. After supper I decided to try once more before going to bed and taking the torch walked to the bottom of the garden where the dark trees swayed in the wind above the Black Burn. The water sang a mournful song, suiting my mood and the small bats fluttered low like aimless butterflies of night above the fields.

"Jake, Jake, where are you? Just answer and I'll forgive you for wandering off. I'll even forgive Mother for letting you out. Come with me to your shed. No tawny owl will frighten you there with its awesome screech. I've got a piece of cheese for your supper and you can fall asleep on my arm. Where are you, answer you black-hearted ruffian?"

The air was silent except for the little bats squeaking madly as they chased insects.

You should not be flying, wizened winged mice. Crawl back into your musty domains and leave the skies to the real birds and one in particular, my friend Jake.

I turned wearily to go back when a faint, pathetic caw emerged from under Jake's own shed. I lay face downwards on the grass and shone the torch. There he was, dusty and dishevelled, not sitting up but crouched low in the damp earth. I reached in and pulled him out. For the first time in his life he pecked viciously at my fingers, hissing and raising the feathers of his neck. I nearly wept. Both his legs were broken and he couldn't stand.

Father would know what to do, he always did, and I carried Jake gently back to the house. Father shook his head when he saw the bird. Both legs were broken between the foot and the next joint.

"We'll try to splint them but ah hae ma doots it'll work," he said'

I held Jake upside down. He was outraged at being held this way and struggled to get free. Father put two small sticks up the sides of each leg and bound them firmly with a bandage.

"Try that and we'll see hoo he gets oan."

I took Jake back to the shed and placed him gently on the floor. Looking smaller than usual and defenceless, he fell over several times but at last he managed to balance when I packed some hay round about his legs for support. He closed his eyes in exhaustion. Fearful of what I would find the following morning, a Saturday, I got up early and ran to the shed. Jake lay crouched on the floor, the hay scattered wide, legs bent awkwardly, already the bandages nearly ripped off with his beak. He cawed feebly in recognition, tongue flecked with blood. One splint might have worked, but not two. Perhaps the muscles at the top of his legs were also damaged.

Father appeared at the door.

"It's nae yis, son, we'll hae tae put him away."

I wept bitterly, "Gie it anither try," but knew it was hopeless.

"Go doon tae the hoose, ah'll see tae it massel," Father said.

I ran, then, ran for miles, down by the Black Burn, along the Great North Road, on and on trying to punish my body so that by sheer physical effort I could perhaps erase the memories flapping in my mind. Jake splashing in his bath, sipping tea noisily like an uncouth old man, hammering away at my teeth or sitting quietly, head cocked to one side and a puzzled expression in his eyes. One memory stood out above all others, though, calling his name and watching him soar down, free and graceful, to land on my shoulder and nibble delicately at my ear lobes, crooning a bird song of love.

I stayed away for two hours, running till exhausted then walking for a while before returning home. They never asked where I had been. Mother just heated up my breakfast, and placed it before me. I knew without asking that Father would have wrung the bird's neck as if he was a domestic fowl and buried it behind the shed where other family pets lay.

Whispers began to reach my ears. Some boys had been seen with catapults in the field near our shed. Pud was one of them and, of all people, Neep. Pud was an obvious suspect, mean and treacherous, but Neep? He was with us when we had obtained Jake from the crags and didn't seem the type who would harm a defenceless bird. I stopped him in the street the next time we met and said "Di yi ken who killed ma jackdaw?"

"It wisnae me onywye," he muttered, but he kept his eyes on his shoes and I sensed that he was involved. I didn't waste time asking Pud. His lies would have been more numerous than a tinker's dog's fleas. Craw's guess was that the three boys involved were Pud, Neep and Erchie Duncan, a boy from a nearby farm.

I scrubbed the shed from top to bottom trying to remove all traces of Jake, taking down the perches and sweeping the last particles of sawdust from the floor. A large white patch defied all efforts, directly under the centre of his favourite roosting perch. The hardest task was picking out all the small trinkets from cracks and ledges. These included two shiny buttons, a nail, toothbrush, washer, elastic band, hairpins and a pea-less whistle, worthless objects but the worldly possessions of Jake the jackdaw.

"Here," my Father said and handed me a small cardboard box. I opened the lid and a white whiskered nose emerged.

"Ah'm no wantin a moose," I said disgustedly.

The mouse climbed out and ran confidently on to my hand. He was certainly attractive, white, with red eyes, a real albino. Though no substitute for Jake, he was a living vibrant creature looking for an owner.

"Puir wee sleekit cowerin beastie," Father said hopefully.

"Ah suppose ah'll hae tae keep it then," I muttered resignedly.

I loved making boxes and Pinky, as I named him, would have the finest box available. Soon it was ready, a hinged lid at the top, two compartments separated by a wall of plywood with an opening and a window in the larger of them covered with fine gauze. Pinky proved to be an interesting pet, inquisitive, agile and friendly.

After a few months I went to the pet shop in Dunfermline and bought him a mate. Their union was fruitful, and soon I had to widen the opening to the nesting chamber as the expectant doe started to get stuck half way through due to the increasing bulk.

I fed the mice twice a day, in the morning before school and about nine o'clock at night. It was a bit eerie going down to the bottom of the garden in the dark so I usually took Lucky the dog with me. He was always interested in the shed with its exciting animal smells and rustlings. Once inside it was warm and cosy after I lit a candle and sat on a bale of hay to feed the mice.

Holding Pinky in my hand, I offered him a piece of cheese and he gripped it in his small delicate hands and nibbled away contentedly. Like hundreds of boys before me, I suppose, I only knew one poem about a mouse apart from the nursery, rhyme Hickory, Dickory Dock, 'To a Mouse' by Burns, and I spoke snatches to him as he ate. "Ah've nae daimen ickers but plenty o cheese."

Any resemblance to this white, pink-eyed pampered pal on my palm and Burns' terrified field mouse must be purely coincidental. I had even, Eastern style, chosen his bride for him and he had accepted her gladly, even eagerly, complete faith in the wisdom of my choice. One night I locked the shed as usual and returned to the house. There was no sign of the dog so I shouted once or twice then went in and forgot all about him.

In the morning as I walked up the path a frantic howling started up. I had locked Lucky in the shed all night and he had nearly torn the door off with his scraping and scratching to get out. Father was furious.

"Ah widni hae geen ye the yis o the shed if ah thocht ye widnae look efter it."

It would be added to his fund of stories for future recital - "The bloomin door wis nearly torn aff its hinges bi gum, the dug wis that desperit tae get tae the toilet."

Certainly the shed was superior to most of the corrugated iron and makeshift doo cribs round about, joiner made at the Co-operative of weather boarding, and creosoted yearly. An aristocratic shed among lesser sheds and now permanently dog damaged. Lucky and I were in disgrace and I banned him from future nocturnal visits.

A few nights later I fed the mice as usual. The doe was very fat now and would have her young soon. In the candle glow I felt the proud protector of the happy expectant couple of romantic rodents. Scratching on the roof of the shed gave me a sudden fright. The dog wasn't with me now and Braewell Cottage was thirty yards away. The unmistakable voice of Pud floated down. "The shed door's open, let's hiv a look inside."

Pud was up to one of his favourite games, climbing up the wall then jumping on to the shed roofs or sometimes from shed to shed if close enough. He had arrived at an opportune time. I still missed Jake tremendously. Every time a jackdaw called from the trees at the Black Burn I heard his echo. The deep furrows in the door reminded me of Father's disapproval. I was lonely, in disgrace, and a fat object I could transfer my anger to crawled like a slug about the roof of our shed. Pud was bigger and stronger than I was but an interloper on our territory.

Another whisper. "Hiv ye ony matches Erchie?"

So. Erchie Duncan, two brave jackdaw killers together. Somewhere, in my chest a drum beat rapidly and my fists clenched in tension. I quickly blew out the candle and stepped softly to the side of the door. Pud struck a match and came into the shed cautiously, blinking like a sleepy owl, the small flame of the match held in front. All my pent up anger exploded and I punched him on the side of the jaw as hard as I could. Pud howled in fright and terror then flew down the path as fast as his fat legs could carry him, leaving Erchie to face unknown horrors on the roof. A frantic scuffling told of his departure. I waited for several minutes then opened the door slightly and looked out. All was quiet.

"That's sorted him," I whispered to the mice. I walked slowly down the path, then started to march, chest up, arms swinging, feeling happier than I had done for days. Ah, revenge was sweet indeed.

Soon young mice ran about the box, leaping and tumbling with great dexterity using their tails like another limb, and I had to make more boxes to accommodate them. The mice colony grew to about fifty as they unashamedly struck up incestuous relationships. The shed began to sound like a circular saw as dozens of mice gnawed at the same time.

Escape proof boxes were hard to devise and holes appeared with monotonous regularity. I patched many of the boxes with scraps of zinc but couldn't keep pace with the restless rodents. Most of the boxes stood on a table at the back of the shed and I partly solved the problem by placing boxes with holes in the sides against the walls of the shed and the smell and occasional taste of creosote at the seams deterred all but the gourmets. Some persistent gnawers still escaped and a woman a few doors away complained.

"Hiv ye still goat they white mice laddie? Ah caught twoh in the mouse trap where ah keep the meal in the hen shed."

Some mated with their wild counterparts and their brown and white offspring were seen in the hen sheds years afterwards. In the wild, no doubt, a natural catastrophe would have taken place in the colony to limit expansion and, in captivity, my sisters took a hand. As with Jake, the tragedy took place when I was training, and late in getting home.

After placing the boxes carefully on the floor my sisters had carried the table out of the shed to play table tennis on the lawn. Unfortunately the holes in the sides were now exposed. I took one horrified look at the happy game in progress, then rushed up the garden path. Mice were everywhere, on the floor, climbing up the walls, running along the roof joists, sniffing, twitching, squeaking, lashing their tails in a frenzy of freedom.

Many were does with young in the nesting boxes I tried to give them time to settle down and placed food in the boxes, but it was hopeless. Some bucks started to fight with each other and the squeaking intensified, others attempted to mate with the does. It was clearly a job for a pied pier and I had no magic flute. Craw with his chanter? No I didn't think that would work. I put the bucks back into separate boxes first, to stop the indiscriminate promiscuity. The mother does still wouldn't return to their own boxes, glorying in their freedom like a group of bored housewives having a night out. Knowing of no way to lure them back, I grouped all the nesting boxes together, placed all the does on a lid in the centre and as soon as one showed the slightest interest in a box, knocked it in and closed the lid.

"If yir no their mither, ye kin be their foster mither."

After all, that's what happend to the evacuees in the village, given a substitute mother with very little explanation or warning. In the morning I fearfully looked on a mouse massacre. Inside the nesting boxes, dead and half eaten young lay in disarray, having been killed either by their disturbed mother or their substitutes. In one box, the naked offspring had been bitten cleanly in half or through the necks. There seemed so many pieces that out of morbid curiosity I laid them on a big flat stone at the edge of the path, lining up a top and a bottom. Fifteen mice lay in a row, a record for me as a breeder if they had lived.

Mice of course breed at a tremendous rate with a gestation period of only three weeks and a colony builds up very quickly. Mice were not the pets for me, I decided. They had their attraction but also a cannibalistic streak. I had been bitten often, especially by one bad tempered old buck. Perhaps he fancied himself as a man eating mouse. I advertised them in the Post Office at one shilling each and at that price they were snapped up, boys arriving with shoe boxes, tea caddies and other containers. The lucky ones got a nesting box thrown in too. Soon the shed was empty, but their characteristic sweet smell lingered on for a long time afterwards. Burns had summed it up well. 'The best laid plans o mice and men gang aft agley.'

GROWING UP

Pud was mellowing, no doubt about that. He didn't hate everyone any more. He was growing and so were the girls in his class. He could see that, and was forever combing his hair now and examining his spots at the mirror. "Ye'll wear that lookin glass done," his mother often remarked. Perhaps some girl would fancy him. After all, even a toad finds a mate. He joined us more on our trips now, trying to make himself agreeable, though Pud being pleasant was like someone else being belligerent.

Winter was nearly over and the Gala Day was not too far off in June. At the end of March the rains came first, lashing the window panes, forming great puddles in the fields and bringing out the damp patches in the walls of Braewell. It seemed to us that it would never stop raining as it kept us awake at night, pattering like mice on the slates and causing a miniature waterfall from the broken rone outside our bedroom window.

Then, one morning, all was silent. I looked out of the window and a long thin dagger of ice bisected my view. A severe frost had come suddenly during the night and the fields were grey and stiff in its grip.

I dressed quickly and ran outside. There was a layer of ice on the garden puddles and Pud's doo was muttering hunger calls in its dingy crib. Pud came out, heavy eyed and sullen, with a bowl of bread and milk. Craw appeared from the field next to the Black Burn.

"The crater's frozen over," he shouted, "but it's still too thin to stand on."

"We'll try it tomorrow," I shouted back.

The crater should have been filled in. The rains had turned it into a marsh, deep sticky mud in places, steep, slippery slopes, and yellow clayey water. Craw and I had braved the rain once just to get out of the house for a while, and squelched down to the crater. We kept a respectful distance away. One slip and those slopes would roll you into the yellow pool at the bottom. We were content to throw in big stones from a few steps back. But now it was different, frozen, and we could slide down the sides and perhaps walk across the ice.

All the children had been warned to keep away from the crater but this only added to its attraction and it was the only bomb crater in Fife to our knowledge. The next day it was still bitterly cold and on the way to school the ice in the puddles easily took our weight.

"The crater shid be aw richt noo," Craw said, as he hacked at a puddle with his heel making little impression on it. After tea that day Jackie arrived and we gave Craw a shout.

"Haw, Craw, ir ye comin oot?"

"Aye, ah'll be there the noo," he replied.

Pud was bored and decided to foist his company on us, with some encouragement from his mother.

"C'mon noo boys, ye kin aw play thegither. Dinnae leave wan oot."

The air felt slightly fresher as we walked down the fields and a chaffinch somewhere offered a few hopeful notes, 'Spring, where are you?'

The crater loomed ominously, an insult on the landscape, its protective fence already rotten and broken in places. We clambered down carefully and tried a tentative foot on the ice. It seemed firm and reasonably thick. Craw walked slowly over the surface first and pronounced it safe. Soon, taking short runs, we slid across the crater, glad to get past the centre, where the ice appeared blacker than the rim. Jackie produced an old pair of ice skates, the kind you fasten on with straps. Craw demanded first shot.

"C' mon Jackie, leader first."

"Awricht," Jackie meekly submitted. Craw sat down and we helped to strap on the old rusty skates.

"Watch hoo it's done," he grinned and half walked, half skated round the crater.

"He thinks he's Sonja Henic," Pud sneered.

Becoming more confident Craw lifted each foot in turn, a bit higher and even slightly sideways in something approaching the right action. We gave him the rink to himself. It didn't look too safe to me and the skates were forming deep furrows in the surface of the ice, which groaned occasionally in protest.

"C'mon Craw, gie's a shot," Jackie shouted.

Craw nodded in agreement. His ankles were aching with the unaccustomed movements.

Pud, who normally would have been protesting his claims, didn't want to risk his weight on the ice, so contented himself uttering abuse. "Yir a lot o show affs," he sneered in safety.

Craw skated clumsily towards us over the dark patch in the centre. He went down so quickly it was unbelievable. The crater swallowed him like a trout taking a fly and the ice re-formed immediately as if nothing had happened.

Only a jagged cross marked the spot where Craw had disappeared. Pud was the first to move. He discovered a hidden courage no one suspected was there, and Craw was the only brother of a sort he had. Grabbing a post from the ruined fence he started smashing a channel through the ice to the centre, wading in, reaching forward occasionally to test the depth. He progressed a few yards then his wellington boots started to sink in the mud and already he was thigh deep. Pud didn't give up. He hauled one leg at a time out of the boots and moved forward rising slightly as he reached a large stone jutting from the bottom of the pool. He roared at us to fetch help as he prodded with the post. Jackie raced fast to the farm for a rope, while I ran back to Braewell.

A crowd came running down the field, Spike leading, my father hobbling along as fast as he could manage near the tail end. As they arrived at the crater, Jackie appeared, breathless, with a long thick rope. Pud was now stuck at the far end of the stone, face white and stiff, up to his waist in broken ice and water. Spike moved towards him, rope tied round his chest. A line of men stretching right up the slope held on to the rope and fed it out as required.

Only Spike could move forwards in the mud, the man next to him tried valiantly but quickly became stuck, like a fly on sticky paper. Spike grabbed Pud by the wrists and pulled hard. He came out with a great squelch to be passed from man to man to the bank. The men in the water started to break the ice with fence posts to widen the channel. The ice now looked pitifully thin. Spike was slowly sinking.

'Heave, heave,' and like a tug o war team the men hauled him to the side in spite of his protests. One of them produced a flask of whisky and Spike drank some gratefully getting a little colour back into his cheeks. "I'm going in again," he said slowly and carefully.

"Dinnae be daft," a man cried, "He's been under quarter o an oor noo. It's hopeless."

Spike just got up in reply and waded in again, the channel much wider now with small pieces of ice floating on the surface. It was getting darker and the air was definitely much fresher with the beginnings of a slight drizzle.

A crowd stood round the crater, silent, helpless. Spike was now up to his chest, scything the water with his great arms, trying desperately to maintain body heat and at the same time probe for the boy if within reach. It was hopeless. I don't think Spike gave up. Again the men decided for him and hauled him in like a roped log, for once the strong man mute, limp and helpless. Father had wrapped Pud in his overcoat and I was sent running to Braewell.

"Hiv they got him yet?" Mother whispered.

"Naw, it's too late onywye. Yiv tae run a bath wi hoat water fir Pud, he's aboot dade wi the cauld, Dad says."

When they arrived, Father stripped off all Pud's clothes and, after checking the temperature, lowered him gently into the bath. His mother, just back from visiting friends, came in distraught, not knowing whether to stay with her son or run to the crater. She waited until she saw that he was all right then ran down the field. Mother gave us hot tea and a sandwich after Pud was dried and dressed in some of my clothes, then Father and I returned to the crater.

It was very dark now and a circle of torches marked the hole. Someone had lit a fire to warm the workers and spectators, using the last of the broken fence. The flames rose and fell, crackling and hissing with the drizzle, bringing the only touch of warmth to the scene of desolation. It was unreal, a dream, unbelievable that Craw was still under. I half expected him to appear at my side, grinning like a monkey, asking what all the fuss was about.

Even with the torchlight, the water was terribly black, the broken ice resembling jagged teeth, in a great maw that had swallowed our friend with the yellow hair.

He couldn't be gone, that swashbuckling buccaneer. He was indestructible, a rock. But he was gone - gone with part of our childhood, for in his going we were a little bit older, a little bit wiser. Craw had come to the village to escape the Clyde bombardment, but a bomb had claimed him after all, indirectly, a few years after it was dropped. The men now had a heavy ladder from the farm stretched right across the crater and Bertie Black crouched on it, probing the water with a long pole. The police had arrived and were keeping the crowd back from the edge of the crater. Spike had been taken away in an ambulance. He was all right, though, they told us.

The women left with the younger children except for Pud's mother, who stood slightly apart from the men, silent and immobile. Craw was dragged out at last about ten o'clock.

Fresh posts and barbed wire were stretched round the crater the following week, and the Council workmen filled it in a month later. The dumped earth must have been of poor quality for the grass in the circle always looked thinner and less green than that surrounding. Dandelions grew profusely on the spot, their yellow heads perhaps a fitting reminder of Thomas Edward Crawford, known to us as Craw.

THE GALA DAY

The silver trophies were displayed in the Co-operative Gents' Department window at the Cross a week before the Gala Day. They sparkled like the Crown Jewels on stands dressed with green velvet. I could never pass by without a look, sometimes detouring from school, drawn by their magnetic spell, pressing my face to the window, attempting to read the engraving. Former champions, some now grown up men with families, were immortalised for ever: John Thompson, Alexander Hodge, William Watson. My, he was so fat now he could hardly walk, never mind run. James Penman, aye, he was a runner alright. He saw wee Erchie pinchin his peas and chased him down the street tae warm his lug. Thomas Sinclair - the names went on and on, stopping at 1940 after war broke out, then on until the present day.

What a shame for the runners of the war years, missing their chance of glory. One cup seemed to stand out from the others or perhaps it only appeared to me that way, the Morrel Trophy, presented by my cousin's husband who was a well known accordionist. I imagined myself stepping up to the stage to be presented with it, crowds flocking around.

"If ye win a cup, the men fill it wi beer, pass it around, tak a drink each and gie the winner a sixpence each," Jackie had told me excitably.

The trophy was big too, at least a foot high with a black wooden base, polished to perfection. I could even see my face in it, strangely contorted as if already engaged in the desperate struggle for immortality. I didn't even know if I could hold the trophy if it was filled with beer, my hands would surely shake with excitement. The Morrel Trophy. It sounded so imposing, the others didn't matter.

George Davie the manager of the shop appeared in the window. He gesticulated angrily and his mouth formed the silent words "Go away, you're dirtying the glass."

I would be back tomorrow and the day after tomorrow. Once a familiar figure arrived beside me and gazed intently at the Morrel Trophy. It was Neep. We didn't speak to each other, our enmity and rivalry lying between us like an unseen pocket of black damp. His face too looked contorted in the silver cup, much uglier than mine I thought.

Ah Neep, Neep. I can't punch you into the ground, you're too big and bony but perhaps I can run you into the ground. That week I trained twice and Joe told us to get to bed early at nights to get maximum sleep. This was difficult as the week wore on and excitement grew. On Friday evening I watched some boys practising the high jump over some iron railings surrounding an un dug garden.

"C'mon Jimmy, hae a shot," one shouted.

I hesitated. No jumps were included in the Morrel Trophy, only running.

"Feardie gowk," he laughed.

Normally I would have cleared the three foot fence easily, but I misjudged the jump, my toe caught on the top rail and I tumbled awkwardly into the grass, twisting my right ankle. Father examined me and pronounced the solemn judgement.

"No running fir you tomorrow, ye daft gowk, trying a thing like that."

I pleaded with him, crying bitterly. "Ah've been trainin fir a year fir this."

He was adamant. "You'll ruin that ankle if ye try tae run oan it tomorrow."

That evening he filled up two basins, one with cold water, the other piping hot and made me steep the ankle for a few minutes alternately in each basin. The next morning the swelling had gone down considerably and I managed to walk normally. Father, I realised, really wanted me to run and perhaps bask in the reflected glory if I did well.

He was as disappointed as I was when I had hobbled in the night before. He examined the ankle again critically.

"Well, ye can gie it a try," he said grudgingly, "but mind, ah'm takin ye richt oot o the race if it gets worse."

For the rest of the morning I hid in the bedroom with the hot and cold basins, sneaking through to the scullery occasionally to fill up one with more hot water.

I could hardly believe it was here, the greatest day of the year in Kelty, the Gala Day. It was as well that I kept out of the way in the morning. The house was in a turmoil as Mother fussed over the three girls as they prepared for the parade. She polished shoes, brushed hair, juggled with the iron, looked frantically for the hairpins and safety pins, trying to ignore Father grumbling.

"When ir ye gaun tae iron ma shirt? Hiv ah nae fresh socks."

The bathroom was impossible, either locked or flooded, talcum powder blowing about like a snowstorm, jammed with female forms in various stages of undress, taps running, scent dripping, tempers fraying.

At last they stood in line for Mother's final inspection, three exotic flowers in light fluffy dresses with ribbons in their hair and holding small coloured flags. I peeped in the door, unwashed and unwanted at the moment, a male Cinderella, but surely these apparitions couldn't be my three sisters, not an ugly one among them.

Boys didn't matter much in the parade, it was an occasion for the girls. All the mothers in the village made a special effort to turn their children out well for the Gala Day. No matter how poor the home, the children were dressed immaculately, almost without exception. Some of the mothers must have saved up for months to buy outfits for their offspring. New shoes, hats and ribbons were in evidence, even though the dresses may have been worn before or passed down from older sisters.

Eventually I washed in the scullery, as Father commandeered the bathroom to shave, then dressed quickly in a pair of grey trousers and a white shirt, with white socks and sandshoes. My hair was short after one of Father's special haircuts, so I had no bother combing it. I wasn't to be hampered by wind resistance, he said.

Mother's inspection was brief. "Did ye wash yir neck?"

"Aye."

"Good, that's all of you ready then."

Jackie arrived, knees and hands looking unnaturally white, and I set off with him, carrying my running kit in an old brown bowling bag. We had strict instructions from Joe not to take part in the parade as it was tiring, so we wandered down to the Cross to find a good viewing position. Already people thronged the pavements, soberly dressed in comparison to the children. Word passed from mouth to mouth.

"They're coming oot the School Gates; they're in Bath Street noo; they've turned the corner."

The excitement grew like a living force. You could feel it surging through the limbs pressed against your own, till at last, "Here they come."

The brass band were first, led by Tommy Proudfoot, not a very appropriate name as both his feet had been chopped off in a pit accident and Doctor Muir had threatened to strike him off his panel if he ever led the Brass Band in parades again. Tommy wasn't going to miss the greatest day of the year, though, and he clumped along in his artificial feet, head up, swinging his arms vigorously, the bandsmen behind him helping to blow him forwards with the mass blast of their instruments.

Various groups of Masonic Lodges came next, holding enormous banners with tassels and portraits of historic heroes, blowing along like galleons in full sail. Scouts, Guides and other organisations followed. Then the pipe band, magnificent in highland dress and none more so than Spike, banging away at the big drum, the only man who could march with it, possibly, head back, great chest raised and covered with a beautiful leopard skin. He winked at me as he passed and I flushed with pride at recognition from this splendid figure.

They played a different tune from the brass band, only thirty yards in front but with all the shouting, laughing and cheering, no one seemed to notice. Then came the children, small ones first, eyes sparkling, flags waving, heads swivelling as they searched desperately for familiar faces in the crowd. The children got bigger and bigger ending with the fourteen year old boy school leavers, gawky, spotted, long-trousered youths, not marching boldly like their young brothers and sisters, but slouching, heads down, faintly embarrassed, ignoring the shouts of recognition from their relatives.

"There's oor Tam. Tam, Tam, wir here. He disnae see us. Tam!"

The teachers and Gala Day committee members walked beside their charges in line and encouraging them to roar every ten yards or so "Hip, hip, hooray, the Gala Day's the day." The procession started from the school, marched to one end of the village, turned round back to the centre then down to the park, stretching for over two hundred yards, a long multi-coloured snake.

Shopkeepers either closed their shops or stood in their doorways, waving. Old people on the Main Street opened their windows and leaned out. "Oh, there's auld Mrs. Broon. Who's that wi her? Aunty Jean. Gie her a shout. Aunty Jean, Aunty Jean."

Some bold spirits risked their lives dashing on to the road frantically trying to focus their cameras as the parade bore down on them, the bands, banners, flags, dresses and gaudy streamers forming an amazing kaleidoscope of colour and movement. The crowds surged after the procession as it entered the park and Bath Street became a seething mass of people, some dodging up side lanes to seek short cuts. Ice cream vans followed, blaring their horns in joyful expectation. Inside the park children sat down in their classes to be given a bag filled with a pie, buns and cakes and a bottle of milk. A stout lady helper, talking polite in front of the teachers, roared out, "Sit down, youse two boys or you won't get your pocks."

Jackie and I looked wistfully on the feast. Cakes were a luxury at home but Joe's instructions were clear, a slice of toast and a glass of milk at eleven o'clock on Saturday morning, then nothing else afterwards but a teaspoonful of glucose just before the first race. I hoped Neep was stuffing himself with all the buns he could find.

As the bags burst, scraps lay everywhere on the grass, all the cakes devoured to the last crumb, but pies not quite so popular. The crack of a gun signalled the first race. The children rushed in unison to the ropes and by the same signal, the ice cream vans, crows and seagulls, waiting like hyenas on the sidelines, rushed in to claim their respective prey.

A small boy's pudgy face disappeared behind an enormous ice cream cone and a seagull's head plunged into a white paper poke. The ambulance men were more patient. They and their tent always seemed very prominent on the Gala Days but never busy. They stood in black uniforms outside the tent, looking round expectantly, eager to try out their skills, waiting for the disaster that never seemed to happen. A few sprains and the odd bleeding nose was their usual fare, but they were always there, willing, waiting.

The Co-operative van blared out announcements and music from the centre of the field. There were three tunes being played now, 'The Green Hills of Tyrol' by the pipe band 'Annie Laurie' from the Brass Band and 'Twelfth Street Rag' from the Co-op. I suppose that you were expected to go closest to the one you liked best.

An announcement came over the loudspeaker, "The hill runners are starting off now."

No one paid them much attention at this stage. They would be away at least an hour, as they ran to the top of Benarty Hill and back. Later the runners could be seen from the park, tiny dots like sheep scaling the hillside.

Arthur Erskine was the only man who had won the race three years in succession. The only stipulation was that the runners touched the check point at the top, taking any possible route there and back. On the way down Arthur cut quarter of a mile off the race by half running, half rolling down a miniature precipice and arrived triumphantly at the park, barely recognisable under mud, grass, heather and blood. The committee men gave him the cup to keep after the third time and bought another for the competition. Arthur retired after that prompted by an official "Hoo aboot giving the other lads a chance, yi'r unbeatable."

The ambulance men still spoke of him in awed whispers. He was their greatest challenge and they had responded magnificently - he always recovered. When he finally emerged from the tent some children ran away in alarm thinking the curse of the mummy was loose in Kelty playpark.

It was a lovely summer's day and groups of people lounged on the grass. The grandparents found a spot to their liking first of all, and their families gathered round, sons, daughters, grandchildren. Former villagers scattered throughout Britain and overseas made a special effort to return to Kelty on their holidays during Gala week. It was a day to renew old friendships and to make new ones. Most of the professional runners including Joe were away at Braemar Highland Games, but big Bertie Black was there to look after us. The novelty races such as the sack, egg and spoon race were held first before the championship events. At last Bert's chance came. He was desperate to perform in front of his home crowd.

"The obstacle race, open to all comers," the co-op van announced. With his running and jumping skills this should be a walkover. The only thing that bothered him was the tree. Two ropes were suspended from a thick branch eight feet off the ground and the competitors had to climb up the rope, over the branch, then down. He had never been that good at rope climbing.

Crack, the gun went and Bert was off like a hare, twenty yards dash, under a tarpaulin, over the vaulting box, ten yards hopping in a sack, another sprint to the tree. Bert paused, smiling smugly. No one else looked in the race, his nearest rival was struggling with a potato sack. Bert climbed easily, tanned muscles glowing in the sunlight, then made his first mistake. He swung one leg over the branch first, as he would have attempted a roll in the high jump, then tried to swing his body over.

He nearly reached the apex then rolled back to his former position. Bert tried again and again. Suddenly with the violent effort, all the strength left his arms and he was stuck under the branch. "Just like a koala bear," an exile from Australia drawled.

The other competitors climbed the rope beside Bert in turn and followed the example of the first man by pulling their chests over first then the rest of the body. They all breasted the finishing tape and Bert was still up the tree.

The co-op van was driven up and Bert was helped gently on to the roof rack which held the loudspeaker. An ambulance man ran up with the smelling salts and we never saw Bert again that day. Jackie and I went into the pavilion and changed into our running shorts and vest. My spiked shoes were already a tight fit and I couldn't get the right one on with the swelling.

"Run in your bare feet," Jackie suggested, "Your sandshoes might slip on the grass."

We went out trying to avoid Father as he would almost certainly stop me from running now. He would be in the crowd at the finishing line so I was fairly safe.

"The Morrel Trophy, one hundred yards, competitors to the starter."

This was it, the moment of truth. I was basically a sprinter and the one hundred my best race. We lined up.

Jackie, lane one; Neep, lane two; another three boys; then me in lane six. Get to your marks, get set. Out of the side of my eye I caught a glimpse of the smoke before the bang and I was off. Joe had told me to watch out for this. I never caught a glimpse of the other runners and flung myself at the tape.

A committee man caught me expertly in one arm and handed me a card with the other. Number One. Neep was second, Jackie third. We registered our cards at the desk. Father rushed over beaming.

"The ither runners wirni in it," he shouted, ignoring the glances from the other parents there.

He hadn't noticed I wasn't wearing spikes as I was in the lane furthest away from him and had slipped on my sandshoes again. The ankle felt fine.

We had half an hour before the two twenty so Jackie and I strolled round the park basking in the compliments.

"Well done lads. Yir like a pair o whippets." "You better no chase ma dochter."

Even Pud was gracious. After all, I was his next door neighbour and he had quarrelled with Neep.

"Aye, yir no a bad runner," he said to me.

That from Pud was praise indeed. "Dae ye think Joe wid gie me a bit o trainin tae?"

Perhaps he thought if he increased his speed he would never again be at the wrong end of a farmer's pitchfork. I heard him proudly tell another boy. "He steys next door tae me."

The two twenty was announced and we made our way to the start. Neep was already there, grabbing the inside position as he had probably been instructed by his trainer. Father pushed forward and informed the starter that the sawdust line would have to be altered as the outside runner would have further to run than those on the inside. Auld Bob Smith scratched his head at this puzzling mathematical technicality, but willing to recognise a superior logic, moved a flag and scratched a new line in the grass.

"There, will that dae yi noo?"

Father wasn't satisfied though. "They should hiv drawn fir positions," he complained as he limped away.

I knew that both Jackie and Neep tended to improve as the races increased in length so all I could do was to attempt a quick start then try to hold on to the lead. Springing first from the line, I led for two hundred yards, then Neep and Jackie passed me and ran side by side for the tape. They collided slightly ten yards from the finish and Neep surged forwards to take the race. I took advantage of the stumble, found an extra spurt and beat Jackie by inches.

Neep and I were now lying level with five points each. Jackie, rather unluckily, was third with two. Neep was sitting on the grass looking ruefully at a leg. He had a nasty gash caused by Jackie's spikes when they had collided.

I unashamedly felt a surge of elation. We are on equal terms, now, oh killer of crows. My ankle was bearing up well and an ambulance man had put a bandage on it for support. Father couldn't bear to come near me now.

He had noticed the bare feet among the spiked shoes and was torn between wanting to pull me out and being the father of a champion. He was hiding somewhere in the crowd, bursting with suppressed rhetoric and emotions. Mother and my sisters kept out of his way, embarrassed at his constant complaints about the committee, the track, the parents of young children who allowed them to run across the track in front of the runners.

One race to go, the quarter mile. I felt sick with tension and as usual went behind a bush and vomited, feeling better afterwards. The sun had gone down a bit and the last of the hill runners had returned from Benarty. A faint drizzle of rain started, no more than a gentle touch on the brow. Mary McIntosh, who had just won the junior girls trophy, walked shyly over. Her eyes were as clear and sparkling as the Golden Linn and she exuded a faint aroma of wintergreen, more potent than any perfume.

"Good luck Jimmy."

I nodded my head but couldn't look into her eyes. A boy could easily drown in their depths. A huge shadow swept over me.

"You kin dae it, son," Spike said. "Ah'll fill the cup wi beer if ye win."

With this magnificent kilted figure banging his drum for me, how could I lose?

"The Morrel Trophy, quarter mile," boomed across the park. It was now or never, the climax of a year's training, cold early mornings and misty evenings on forgotten tracks in secret places, joints cracking in protest at the loosening up exercises, the strong smell of liniment and sweat, the harsh voice of Joe giving us exercises "Up, down, up, down, up, down."

He expected us as usual the next week for training. Professionals didn't take training days off in the middle of the games season, and we were the nucleus of his future adult school of runners.

The park stood on a high plateau at the edge of the village and I took a last look round the familiar scene – the school, where I had spent hours wrestling with sums and dreaming of the bright streams of the Gairney and Queichs; Cleish Crags in the distance with minute specks flickering above; Benarty, tall and majestic guarding Loch Leven; a small group of trees and the red pantiles of Black Dub; and just beyond the park, the chimneys of Braewell and cows grazing peacefully in the fields next to the Black Burn. I turned my back on the scarred landscapes to the east and south. Perhaps one day it would bloom again and the bleak slag tips vanish for ever.

As I walked to the starting point a softly muted rainbow shimmered for a moment then vanished. A good omen I thought. Just as it appeared to Noah. It must be for me,

Neep didn't go to the Sunday School. We didn't crouch down for the quarter mile. As boys we looked on this as a distance race, not a sprint, and stood upright, forward foot on the line.

"Now Neep, let's see what you're made of."

We are all scarred warriors now. I've a bandage on my ankle, you've a big plaster stuck on your leg, Jackie has his usual selection. Don't fall Neep, these black crows sitting on the school wall are waiting to flap to you if you do. They haven't forgotten Jake.

Only he or I could win the trophy now. We had five points each and Jackie two.

"Ir yi wantin ony mair stickin plaister, boys?" a voice drawled from the crowd, "There's some empty spaces yit."

A harsher voice spoke up. "Shut up, gie the loddies a chance ir ye'll be needin some yirsell."

"Quiet noo, lads," said auld Bob Smith, "they'll no hear the gun."

He birled it on his fingers as if he was Hopalong Cassidy, to the danger of the crowd who drew back in haste.

Get Set. A slight lean forward and a big gulp of air. Crack! This time I felt I had really been shot in the pit of the stomach, such was the tension. This was Jackie's best race. I held the lead for over a lap then he passed me, with Neep, loping like a wolf, soon after. My ankle now throbbed with pain. Perhaps Father was right. If I damaged it today I might never run again in competition. But 'if ifs and ands were pots and pans there'd be nae need fir tinkers' Concentrate, keep going. I increased speed and caught up with the two leaders. My ankle protested hotly at the sudden surge but I was there, challenging Neep and Jackie. They ran side by side now, neither giving way with Jackie having the advantage on the inside. Good old Jackie. He found a reserve of strength, took the lead and headed for the tape.

Neep was still three yards ahead of me with fifty to go, those big ungainly arms and legs flaying like windmills, a hard obstacle to pass. I felt the pain all over now, in my legs, chest and head, pounding, throbbing, stabbing. Surely I was gaining slightly, that turnip head growing bigger. Twenty yards or was it twenty miles?

The rainbow appeared again, but closer now, in fact it seemed in front of my eyes, winking, flashing in its splendour, forming an arc between me and the Morrel Trophy, the pot of gold at the end of the rainbow. Just beyond the tape, the Pipe Band was playing Craw's favourite. 'The Rowan Tree,' the haunting music soaring upwards, like a whaup to the dark summit of Benarty.

'Oh Rowan Tree, Oh Rowan Tree, ye'll aye be dear to me.'

I ran towards the sound, wrapped in the rainbow, reaching forwards blindly, not knowing whether I had won or lost.

ABOUT THE AUTHOR

Jim Douglas, pictured here in front of his mural in Kelty Library, is a poet, songwriter, artist and silversmith. His songs have been recorded by over a dozen well –known artistes and sung by many others.

His first book *Dugs, Doos and Dancing* was a best seller, and his paintings and cartoons have found homes in places as far apart as mining villages and royal palaces. He is in great demand as a public speaker, and has featured several times on Radio Heartland and Radio Tay. His Radio Scotland appearances include The Reel Blend, Roads of Summer and Travelling Folk.

WINDFALL BOOKS

Poetry Collections:
Having It All
Pointing At Rainbows
Black Dog Blues
Butterfly Love
Playing With Words

Lillian King:
A Railway Childhood
The Last Station
Famous Women of Fife
Sair, Sair Wark, Women and Mining in Scotland
That's Entertainment – 100 Years of Dunfermline Opera House
Building The Bridge

Morris Allen & Tim Tyler:
In Search of The Scottish Wildcat

Jim Douglas:
Dugs, Doos and Dancing

Thomas Cotter:
Expendable

David Lockhart RSW:
Unforgotten